How to be Fit and Young?

Published by
Lotus Press

Preface

Only a person with healthy mind can have a healthy body, and only a person with a healthy psyche can have a healthy physique as well. Numerous guidelines are there in this modern world to remain fit and young. However, the majority of them adopt merely artificial methods which create life-long health problems. In order to remain healthy and fit one needs impose upon oneself several restrictions. It includes regular and guided exercise, abstaining from intoxicants, disciplined food habits and balanced amount of sleep, entertainment, work and passtime activities. These all apart, one should learn to take all positive and negative happenings normally, as these come one's way.

Considering the extensive efforts put into this work, this should prove to be highly useful for all the readers, young and old. It is the best guide for everybody who wants to remain fit and young.

—Author

Contents

1

Health and Fitness

Health and Fitness is a very important factor in all physical activities and Martial Arts is no exception. Therefore, in this chapter we will be covering all aspects of physical and mental training. "Before partaking in any physical activity get a full medical check-up from your physician."

In 1993, the Centre for Science in the Public Interest (CSPI) attracted extensive media attention when it reported that Chinese restaurant food is unhealthy. A meal of kung pao chicken, the centre claimed, is comparable to "four McDonald's quarter pounders." In the months that followed this news, the CSPI focussed on several other types of food—including Italian food, Mexican food, and movie-theatre popcorn—that, according to the centre's findings, contained unhealthy levels of salt and fat.

The centre declared that fettuccine Alfredo is "a heart attack on a plate," that eating "chile rellenos is like eating a whole stick of butter," and that a medium-sized container of movie-theatre popcorn with butter-flavoured topping contains "more fat than a bacon-and-eggs breakfast, a Big-Mac-with-fries lunch, and a steak dinner with all the trimmings combined."

In response to this ever-growing list of dangerous foods, Mike Royko, a columnist for the *Chicago Tribune,* undoubtedly expressed the frustrations of many Americans when he wrote, "I can save the Centre for Science in the Public Interest a lot of bother and expense. All it takes is a simple announcement: If something tastes good, it is probably bad.

If something tastes really dull, it is probably good." In a humorous tone, Royko asked, "Who knows where the food nags will strike next? A deli?" Ironically, delis were one of the CSPI's subsequent targets: It proclaimed that an egg-salad sandwich "makes a Dairy Queen banana split look like a diet food."

The CSPI's campaign against unhealthy food and the reaction to it illustrates the uneasy relationship that often exists between health experts and the American public. Health officials—with the help of the news media and advertisers—produce a constant stream of information about the health effects of various foods, beverages, chemicals, drugs, lifestyles, and activities.

These reports ceaselessly implore the public to adhere to dietary and fitness guidelines that are continually being updated, revised, and amended. Because these recommendations are in constant flux—and often contradict one another—frustration such as that expressed by Royko is commonplace. Some people adopt the attitude that because risks are ubiquitous and health problems are unavoidable, it is futile to attempt to alter one's behaviour to avoid the inevitable.

Daniel Minturn, a shipping clerk interviewed by Richard Woodbury in *Time* magazine, succinctly summed up this philosophy as he prepared to eat a cheeseburger: "Everywhere you turn, it's a warning for this and a warning for that. So what's wrong with just now and then going out and enjoying what you want?"

In fact, health experts who challenge the CSPI's claims suggest that Minturn's attitude is the correct one. Elizabeth M. Whelan, the president of the American Council on Science and Health, argues, CSPI's diet advice is "lite" on science and "reduced" in common sense. It overlooks the fact that what is important is one's overall diet, not the occasional consumption of any specific food. The key to healthy eating is a balanced, varied, moderate diet—and there is room in that overall scheme for fettucini and popcorn.

Whelan and others accuse the CSPI of oversimplifying nutritional science. These critics contend that the restaurant foods cited by the CSPI are safe in moderate amounts, and that the CSPI ignores the fact that the degree of risk posed by fat and salt intake varies among individuals.

For example, Jacob Sullum writes in *National Review,* "While too much (salt) aggravates certain kinds of hypertension, there is no medical reason for people in general to avoid it." Similarly, he argues that although "a high-fat diet may increase the risk of heart disease in some people, that does not mean that fettuccine Alfredo, kung pao chicken, and chile rellenos are poison."

Not only do experts debate the dangers posed by fat levels in particular foods, they also disagree about the risks and benefits of different types of fat. The food guide pyramid developed and issued by the U.S. Department of Agriculture (USDA) in 1992 recommends using all fats and oils "sparingly." However, according to Michael Mason, a staff writer for *Health* magazine, this advice is misguided because it fails to differentiate between kinds of fat.

While saturated fat has been linked to heart disease, Mason notes, monounsaturated fat may actually benefit the cardiovascular system. Mason argues that by lumping all fats and oils together, the USDA calls for cutting olive oil, which is a source of monounsaturated fat. Simultaneously, according to Mason, while the pyramid advises cutting fats and oils, it allows for two to three servings per day of red meat, which is high in saturated fat. To rectify these inconsistencies, Mason endorses an alternative pyramid that was developed in 1994 by the Harvard School of Public Health, Oldways Prevention and Exchange Trust, and the World Health Organisation. Based on the traditional Mediterranean diet, the new pyramid recommends eating red meat only a few times a month and calls for daily use of olive oil.

Along with contradictory information on nutrition, the public also receives mixed signals on exercise. For example, during the 1970s and 1980s, experts recommended that Americans engage in vigorous exercise for a minimum of thirty minutes a day, five days a week.

In 1993, however, new guidelines were released jointly by the U.S. Centres for Disease Control and Prevention (CDC) and the American College of Sports Medicine (ACSM). The CDC and the ACSM called for moderate exercise and said that the recommended daily amount of activity could be "accumulated in short bouts" rather than during one workout, as was previously recommended. Then, in 1995, a study authored by IMin Lee, an assistant professor of medicine at the Harvard School of Public Health, concluded that vigorous exercise—but not moderate exercise—was associated with greater longevity, suggesting that only vigorous exercise could help people live longer. Reflecting the public's confusion, an Associated Press article reporting on Lee's study began, "Run! No, walk. No, run!"

The uncertainty caused by such contradictory information can lead some people to become discouraged and to adopt a careless attitude about their personal health and fitness. However, amid the cacophony of competing recommendations, a few generalisations can safely be made. Most experts agree that some exercise is better than no exercise, and most agree that the best diet is a varied one low in saturated fat. In *Health and Fitness: Opposing Viewpoints* authors examine diet, exercise, and other things for instances. What Behaviours Pose the Greatest Health Risks and Benefits? Are Exercise and Weight-Loss Treatments Beneficial? Are Alternative Therapies Viable? Is the Health Care Industry Effective? Throughout these chapters, issues that affect the health and fitness are discussed and debated.

Maybe you've never done much in physical fitness, but you would like to learn about it and see what's involved. Or maybe you have been exposed to some aspects of exercise, but don't feel that what you learned was balanced and comprehensive enough. Maybe you've noticed signs of aging and disuse in your body, and want to do something about it.

Most books, videos and television programmes dealing with health and fitness are narrow in who they're aimed at, the methods they promote and the information they provide.

Aging and longevity research has shown that physical exercise is the most important single factor for a healthy long life. In the many thousands of years of human evolution, it's only during the most recent fragment of time that large numbers of us have had the dubious luxury of inactivity.

We live under sedentary conditions that are alien to the way our internal organs, skeleton and musculature evolved. Exercise returns us to a more natural condition. Reaction times and hormones tend to remain at more youthful levels for physically active people.

You don't need long gut-wrenching workouts to benefit. You need a persistent long-term programme of moderate intensity. Fitness requires some effort on your part. Don't let anybody tell that you can get health and fitness gains without some effort. However, a well-directed programme will minimise the effort and maximise the gain.

Few Questions Related to Health and Fitness:

- What are the three basic categories of exercise and their priorities for health and fitness?
- Considering the diet that most people eat, what are the main problems?
- When it comes to making adjustments to improve our fitness and health, how long should we continue these before we can resume our old bad habits? A few months? A couple years? Until we find somebody to date? The rest of our lives?

Read on if you would like the answers to those questions.

Exercise Answers

Physical exercise falls into three categories:

1. The leading priority is cardiovascular fitness, which is exercise aimed at the heart muscle. The main concern in fitness is to stay alive and a strong heart helps in that regard. Cardio-vascular fitness exercises work large muscle groups in a light persistent manner so that those muscles demand increased blood and pumping action from the heart. Typical examples are running, biking, and aerobics. Research indicates that cardio-vascular (CV) sessions lasting about 30 minutes every day are sufficient for most fitness purposes.

   Most people are unaware that for each individual there's window of exertion that CV workouts should fall within to get the desired effects. You'll be shown how to determine the intensity level of exercise necessary for you to get an optimum conditioning effect from your CV exercise sessions.

2. The next priority in physical fitness is stretching the major muscle groups and strengthening the lower back. The value of a long life is diminished if a person is stiff, partially immobile or in nagging back pain. It's

remarkable how little exposure and emphasis this point gets. The only equipment you need is your living room floor. Stretching exercises should be done a few minutes daily.

Keeping the lower back muscles flexible and strong should be a high priority in any fitness plan. There's a tendency for men to discount stretching exercises and concentrate on strength training. That's not smart. Physical prowess is greatly enhanced by limberness. In most sports, the best athletes have a flow of motion that is simply not possible with stiff weak back muscles.

3. The last fitness priority is strength training. This is the type of exercise that gets the most attention. Weightlifting can make you look good but it shouldn't be the first priority in fitness training. A barbell set, a weight bench and a good workout plan are all that's needed. Used with common sense, working out with barbells is as safe as any other method. The strength training routine takes about 30 minutes, every day. Over a period of months, the average person can improve their strength greatly and make their appearance more youthful and attractive. This applies to women as well as men. Women normally don't gain muscle mass like men sometimes do with intensive weight training—but they do gain a more healthy, youthful athletic appearance.

The overall plan is to work out 5 or 6 days a week for about 30 minutes each time. You alternate the days between cardiovascular and weight-lifting exercises, with a little overlap that will be described later. In addition, every day you spend several minutes doing stretching routines. In addition to exercise, many people should adjust their diets away from excessive quantities of food, and away from food that is loaded with fat and sugar.

Healthy changes in exercise and diet should be lifelong, not for some limited period of time. Changes that are realistic for a lifetime have to be sensible—not extremist fad-oriented or requiring so much time or effort that they become burdensome and get abandoned. Sensible methods that can become lifelong habits are what you will see here.

Working Out

Exercise in the most comfortable convenient room in your house or apartment. Have a TV and a radio/tape player there, so that you can merge the time with entertainment. It should be a brightly-lit area and if you have children, it will be a good influence on them to see you exercising. Don't confine your work-out area to the basement or garage. The idea is to make it as enjoyable and convenient as possible, and to make it as habitual as possible.

Habit of Fitness

The idea of making fitness a habit is important. People often associate "enthusiasm" with working out and getting fit. There's nothing wrong with bringing enthusiasm to a worthwhile endeavour. However, it's not enough, it usually wanes, and it's really not the key ingredient.

Here's the important thing about a fitness programme—make it a habit. Make it a habit to do your cardio-vascular exercise regularly. Make it a habit to do your stretching exercises daily. Make it a habit to do your weight-training exercises regularly. Make it a habit not to overeat. Habitually steer away from high fat and high sugar foods.

Developing a "fitness habit" is important. The idea is to abandon bad habits, like physical passivity, and get new good ones. Any exercise plan that isn't conducive to becoming habitual is a waste of time. If it's too difficult, or too time-consuming it's not a winner. The plan presented here is something you can make into a permanent part of your daily activities.

Formation of Habit

Habits are developed by means of two basic factors: reward and repetition. When adults make changes in their lives through new behaviour, they have go through the process of forming new habits. Enthusiasm by itself is not enough. It can get you started, but it's not the thing that maintains a change in long-term behaviour.

- As an adult, you have to decide what you want (a reward like looking better and being healthier).
- Determine what you need to do to get it.
- Then start doing it repetitively.

Losing weight and/or building up your muscles are not rewards that will occur immediately—they take at least some months. So the reward is delayed and to a large extent the formation of a new habit in physical exercise and diet depends mostly on repetition. But that's nothing unusual. Many of our habits grow from repetition and delayed reward.

Brushing your teeth several times a day doesn't yield any immediate reward. The payoff is a "non-event"—the dentist not using his drill on you months into the future. But that ephemeral association doesn't deter most people from engaging in dental hygiene.

The delayed reward of looking better and avoiding health problems in the future shouldn't preclude you from forming new habits in the area of physical exercise and diet.

Building habits through repetition is easy. How many times have you driven an often-travelled route without thinking? Sometimes, it can get so habitual that even if you intended to divert off the course to go some place else, you miss the turn off and follow the habitual course. That's the behaviour that you want to get working for you in the areas that you choose.

You want to find it easier to follow your fitness programme, than not to.

Here are some factors and techniques that might help you in developing positive habits.

Favourably Alter Your Environment

If you want to encourage yourself to exercise regularly, then put your equipment in a convenient place. Don't put it down in the basement or in some room you never go into. If you want to stop eating certain types of foods, then throw them out of the kitchen and avoid restaurants where they are served.

Stock up on the kinds of food you intend to eat. If you want to cut down on eating, minimise your time in the kitchen by preparing easy to make things. If you want to encourage yourself to do your cardio-vascular exercises regularly, keep your running shoes, skip rope or whatever equipment you use in plain sight. What you see—you think about. What you think about—you do.

Monitor Your Behaviour

Get a calendar devoted solely to your physical fitness and/or diet programmes. Maintain it daily. Everyday mark down whether you followed the programme, or did not. The days for which you failed should cause you a certain amount of dissatisfaction and impatience with yourself. Remember, repetition over time will make the desired behaviour become easier to fulfil. Lapses just delay and make your goal's achievement more difficult.

Creative Thinking

Get in the habit of imagining and mentally rehearsing what you want to do. Several times a day, whether you are alone or not, take 20 or 30 seconds to imagine seeing yourself and feeling yourself doing your next scheduled workout.

Maybe you find yourself in some irrelevant meeting listening to someone rattling on. Give yourself the luxury of escaping for a moment.

In your "minds eye"...

- See yourself coming home this evening.
- See yourself changing into your work-out clothes.
- See yourself doing your exercises.
- Feel the satisfaction you will have when you've done your workout.

This kind of visualisation works in a couple ways. It's a good method to implant a thought that will recall itself at the right time. But when you add good feelings to the visualisation you not only tend to remember to do it, but actually want to do it.

Generally, when you want to promote a certain activity by thought, it's best to think positively about the benefits that come from carrying out the behaviour, rather than thinking about the negative consequences of failing to do it. In other words—think positively.

Set-up an Intermediate Reward System

The main reward in a physical fitness programme takes some time in coming. However, perhaps there are some things that you particularly enjoy that you can hold as rewards to yourself for following your programme. Perhaps two weeks with no lapses should be rewarded by spending a little more than you normally would to see a good play, or for shopping.

Be Realistic

You often hear about people setting very high goals and then driving themselves to fulfil them. You don't often hear how this can promote discouragement and failure. If you want to lose 15 kg give yourself 15 to 30 weeks to do it in a steady progressive manner. Even if you could lose it faster than that, it's usually unwise to do so.

Crash diets put too much strain on the system. The methods involved in doing them are almost never supportable over the long-term, so people who crash down in weight, almost always vault right back up again.

Similarly, be patient in your muscle strengthening programme. You will probably gain muscle strength quickly the first few months without it showing up very much in the mirror. Don't expect 30 minute weight-lifting sessions every day to result in you looking like a body-builder. However, this type of programme will start visibly showing through in six months to an year. And over the course of several years, the average person will take on an appearance of an obviously fit person.

Support from a Partner?

Can you benefit by teaming up with a partner? The idea is that you encourage your partner if they start slacking off, and vice versa. The problem is that a weak partner will undermine your efforts. In addition, you may wind up disrupting the formation of your work-out habits due to scheduling problems.

You definitely do not want to miss or even alter the timing of your workouts because of difficulties in synchronising two schedules. Schedule disruption's will damage your ability to form the fitness habit. And habit is the key. Most people will be best off developing the fitness habit on their own.

Just Starting Out?

If you're just starting an exercise programme after a long period of inactivity you should take it easy during the first month. The objectives during this beginning period are not to see how strong you are or even to get much of a workout. The priorities are:

1. To slowly accustom your muscles and heart to exertion. Doing too much in the starting phase can lead to serious muscle soreness. Obviously, doing cardiovascular exercise when you are out of shape has the risk of overtaxing the heart, and should be done cautiously and perhaps only after a physical examination by a doctor. Listen to your body, and use good judgement.
2. To learn the proper form of the routines. Do the exercises right, so you get the maximum benefit.
3. To ease into the habit of taking time each day for exercise. Be consistent and use repetition to ingrain a good work-out habit in you.

How you start out on an exercise programme is important. Overdoing things in the beginning can mess the whole thing up. Here's an anecdote about a guy who was in that position.

Weight Machines

Romy had never been particularly athletic even in his high school and college days. He didn't have much of a base of knowledge to go from when his doctor advised him to lose weight and start getting some exercise. He was in his mid '30s, had a pot belly and mild high blood pressure. As part of a new year's resolution he joined an athletic club not far from work and resolved to start spending his lunch-times exercising, instead of in restaurants.

He didn't know quite what to expect from this unfamiliar environment the first day he walked into the work-out room. The place was filled with 20 or 30 machines specialised for exercising everything from the calf muscles all the way up to the neck. Ten or 15 people were in the room busily using the machines and he decided the best thing to do was simply to watch what others were doing and follow on.

After a few tries at the machines, he realised that he had no idea how much weight he should be using for a given exercise. A couple machines he had tried gave too little resistance, while others had so many plates selected that he could barely get one repetition completed (to his embarrassment). All the other guys and girls in the work-out room seemed like old hands at all this, leaving him feeling all the more obvious in his inadequacy. This got his hackles up and he elected to leave early and come back during the mid afternoon when he knew he would have the place more to himself. Then he could experiment with the machines and note what weights to use on each, away from the gaze of amused eyes.

As he had expected, the place was nearly empty when he returned. The aggravation of his earlier experience spurred him on in his determination to conquer the machines. He went from contraption to contraption experimenting with the number of weight plates for which he could manage to make the cams and levers move along their prescribed paths.

His enthusiasm for the idea of getting healthy and fit grew as he drove himself to conquer every machine in the weight room. The full spirit of it all impelled him to forcing himself not to give up until he couldn't get out another repetition on each and every apparatus. Finally, he went to the showers feeling that he had really accomplished something. He had used his enthusiasm to confirm his commitment to himself to improve his health!

Unfortunately, while Romy's enthusiasm gave him over to a spate of beginners' euphoria, his long-neglected muscles were soon to burst the bubble. They didn't appreciate such rough treatment after years of non-use. Romy felt pain in every bit of his body the next morning. It was to be over a month before he went anywhere near that weight room again, and then only after he had read everything and queried everybody he could on the right way to go about weight training. He recalled that when he had learned to drive a car, like everyone else he had taken it one careful step at a time. He hadn't just jumped behind the wheel and gone out on the freeway during rush hour.

Fat: Fat, perhaps no other word in our language is despised as much, nor focused on so intensely. Peoples are obsessed about fat—body fat—and how to get rid of it. We have been conditioned to view health and fitness in strictly black (fat) and white (fit) terms: A "fat" body cannot possibly be fit and healthy. This fat-versus-fit dichotomy, made popular in the 1970s with the publication of fitness guru Covert Bailey's "Fit or Fat?", has become the mantra of many a fitness and health professional. You don't have to read any more than the title to grasp the fundamental message of this perennial best-selling fitness bible: A person is either fit, or fat—but not both.

The implications of this myopic fitness philosophy are obvious: The road to a fitter and healthier body is a very narrow one indeed. In order for a fat person to become fit and healthy, that person must lose weight and become lean. This of course implies that "lean" is inherently good and "fat" is inherently bad. Not only is this lipophobic paradigm overly simplistic, it does not stand up against a substantial amount of medical and scientific evidence.

Obesity-Heart Disease Link Challenged

Take coronary artery disease (atherosclerosis), for example—the number one killer in the developing countries. Conventional wisdom tells us that obesity itself is a major cause of clogged arteries—the rationale being that more fat on the body equals more fat in the blood stream equals more fat build-up in the arteries. However, most of the studies that have looked at the relationship between body weight (or body fat) and atherosclerosis—via coronary angiography or by direct examination of artery disease at autopsy—find that fat people are no more likely to have clogged arteries than thin people.

In some instances results entirely opposite to conventional wisdom are observed. For example, in U.S. when researchers at the University of Tennessee evaluated coronary angiograms of more than 4,500 men and women, they found that the risk of having a clogged artery actually decreased as body weight increased. In other words, it was the fat men and women who had the cleanest arteries. Although this finding is exceptional, the preponderance of angiography studies of this nature do undermine the notion that obesity inevitably results in clogged arteries.

Furthermore, the findings from angiography studies are consistent with countless autopsy studies—dating back to the middle of this century—of the link between body weight (or body fat) and arterial disease. The large-scale International Atherosclerosis Project, for example, conducted in the late 1950s and early 1960s, concluded after analysing 23,000 sets of coronary arteries—obtained at autopsy—that no measure of body weight or body fat was related to the degree of coronary vessel disease. The obesity-heart disease link is just not well supported by the scientific and medical literature.

Thinner not Necessarily Healthier

The same could be said for the notion that thin people are healthiest and can expect to live longer than everybody else. Contrary to the prevailing medical mindset, the "thin-live-longest" studies frequently cited by the more vocal of the anti-fat crusaders are far outnumbered by studies demonstrating that body weight—aside from the extremes—is not really all that strong a predictor of death rates, or overall health for that matter.

A 1996 publication by researchers at the National Centre for Health Statistics and Cornell University illustrates perfectly. After analysing the results from dozens of published reports on the impact of body weight on death rates, encompassing more than 350,000 men and nearly 250,000 women, the researchers found that moderate obesity (no more than about 22.7 kg. in excess of the so-called ideal body weight) increased the risk of premature death only slightly in men, and not at all in women, during follow-up periods lasting up to 30 years. In fact, the researchers found that thin men—even within the range recommended by the current U.S. government guidelines—had a risk of premature death equal to that of men who were extremely overweight. The researchers warned in their summary comments that "attention to the health risks of underweight is needed, and body weight recommendations for optimum longevity need to be considered in light of these risks."

In America the Metropolitan Life Insurance Company introduced its tables of "ideal" weights in 1942 —the company called them "desirable" weights in 1959, and did away altogether with the terms "ideal" and "desirable" in 1983—we have been operating under the weight loss industry-reinforced assumption that weighing more than what the height/weight charts say we should weigh is a sure sign of poor health and greatly increases risk of premature death. However, the majority of body weight-mortality investigations have shown that weighing 90 pounds, or 30 pounds, or even 50 pounds in excess of the height-weight chart recommendations is associated with little, if any, increased risk of an early check-out.

For example, the current U.S. government guidelines indicate that a 5'4" woman should weigh between 111 pounds and 146 pounds, and a 5'10" man should weigh between 132 pounds and 174 pounds. According to the 1996 study previously mentioned, a 5'4" woman and 5'10" man could weigh close to 200 pounds before their risk of premature death goes up appreciably (excess body weight seems to be riskier in men than in women). This suggests that there are a great many "overweight" Americans—especially women—who are agonising unnecessarily about those numbers on the bathroom scale.

So if being a little fatter than average might not be so bad, and being thin (at least for men) might not be so good, what does this say about body weight and health? If the concept of an ideal weight is little more than statistical fiction, should we just chuck the bathroom scale, kick back on the sofa with a bag of chips in one hand and the remote control in the other, and nestle into total couch-potato-hood? Of course not (although chucking the bathroom scale is probably a good idea). It's just that body weight, and even body fat for that matter, do not tell us nearly as much about our health as lifestyle factors, such as exercise and the foods we eat. Consider the following scenario.

Randomly select a few hundred men and women (matched for age and smoking habits) and divide them into two groups based on body fat: lean and fat. Next take each person's blood pressure, draw some blood and determine each person's serum lipid levels, and have each person perform a glucose tolerance test (to get an idea of each person's insulin sensitivity). You will find, on average, higher blood pressures, unhealthier blood lipid profiles, and poorer glucose tolerance/insulin sensitivity in the group of fat men and women.

Does this mean that the higher body fat levels caused the health problems? No. It just means that you are more likely to find these kinds of metabolic disorders in fat men and women. But associations do not prove cause-effect. Just because you are more likely to observe high blood pressure, elevated blood lipids and glucose intolerance in fat persons does not prove that body fat is the cause of these health problems, nor does it mean that a fat person has to become lean in order to resolve these health problems. The proof of this assertion is quite straightforward. Get these fat men and women to start an exercise programme and eat healthier foods—and see how they do. Numerous research studies have done just that. A few examples are described below.

Weight-related Health Problems

Results from the Dietary Approaches to Stop Hypertension (DASH) clinical trial, published in the New England Journal of Medicine in 1997, proved that blood pressures can be effectively lowered by simple changes in diet, without losing weight. Among 133 men and women with high blood pressure, just eating more fruits and vegetables, and consuming low-fat dairy foods with reduced saturated fat, was sufficient to reduce systolic blood pressure by an average of 11.4 mmHg, and diastolic blood pressure by an average of 5.5 mmHg, within two weeks after changing their diets. The reductions in blood pressures were comparable to those observed with initiation of pharmacotherapy—but without the side-effects which sometimes accompany antihypertensive medications. Most significantly, the blood pressure reductions were achieved without any weight loss.

To prove that it's fat in the diet—and not fat on the body—that is the primary cause of blood lipid abnormalities, such as high cholesterol, researchers at the National Public Health Institute in Helsinki, Finland, placed 54 middle-aged men and women on a low-fat (~24 per cent of total calories) diet for six weeks. Total cholesterol dropped from 263 mg/dl to 201 mg/dl in the men, and from 239 mg/dl to 188 mg/dl in the women. Body weight did decrease modestly, by about 2 pounds.

The subjects were then switched back to their usual diet (~39 per cent of total calories from fat) for six weeks. Total cholesterol levels returned to their original levels—despite absolutely no change in body weight—requiring the researchers to conclude that the fat content of the diet, not weight change, was responsible for the changes in cholesterol levels.

Combined exercise and nutrition programmes have provided even more compelling results, as illustrated by the changes observed in the more than 4,500 men and women who have completed a 3-week stay at the Pritikin Longevity Centre in Santa Monica, California. The Pritikin programme consists of eating a low-fat, high-complex starch, high-fibre diet (with no emphasis on rapid weight loss) and daily moderate-to-vigorous aerobic exercise.

Within three weeks the average cholesterol level dropped from about 234 mg/dl to about 180 mg/dl; low-density lipoprotein cholesterol (the unhealthy kind) decreased from around 151 mg/dl to 116 mg/dl; and triglycerides were reduced by one-third (from 200 mg/dl down to 135 mg/dl).

Pritikin programme participants lowered their blood pressures by an average of 5-10 per cent, and more than one-third of the men and women with high blood pressure were able to discontinue antihypertensive medications. Those with type II (adult onset) diabetes also experienced tremendous improvements: 39 per cent of those taking insulin and 71 per cent of those on oral hypoglycemic agents were able to discontinue medication entirely.

All of these improvements in health profile while on the Pritikin programme were observed within three weeks. Although participants do lose weight (typically about 5 per cent of their initial body weight), statistical analysis indicates that less than 5 per cent of the improvements in health can be attributed to changes in body weight. Most important to the question at hand is the fact that most men and women who enter the programme obese leave the programme obese—but with one major difference: They no longer have the health problems thought to be caused by excess body fat.

Just as risk factors for heart disease can be affected by changes in lifestyle independent of changes in body weight, the actual disease itself can be influenced by lifestyle modification—without changes in body weight. The results of the Cholesterol Lowering Atherosclerosis Study illustrate. Eighty-two moderately overweight middle-aged men with heart disease were placed in a two-year intervention programme designed to reduce consumption of dietary fat. Men who reduced their fat intake to 27.5 per cent of total calories showed no new fatty deposits in their coronary vessels (as determined by examination of coronary angiograms taken before and after the two-year study).

On the other hand, men who failed to make significant changes in fat intake (34 per cent of total calories from fat) didn't do as well—they all showed some evidence of new lesions in their coronary vessels. Because neither group lost any weight during the two-year study, the researchers concluded, in a 1990 article published in the Journal of the American Medical Association, that "the appearance of new [coronary artery] lesions can be influenced without weight change by voluntary selection of acceptable foods."

Health and Longevity

All this evidence suggests that as far as one's health is concerned, lifestyle is far more important than body weight. This goes for longevity prospects as well, as the ongoing—since 1970—Aerobics Centre Longitudinal Study at the Cooper Institute for Aerobics Research, in Dallas, Texas, demonstrates. Data on more than 32,000 men and women indicate that the fittest men and women have the lowest death rates—regardless of what they weigh. In other words, a heavier-than-average person who is physically fit has a better chance of living a long life than does a thin couch potato.

Furthermore, a separate analysis of nearly 10,000 of the men in this study who performed at least two exercise stress tests separated by an average of about 5 years (thereby allowing the researchers to evaluate the impact of changes in physical fitness on subsequent death rates), revealed that improving physical fitness level reduced death rates during the 5+ years of follow-up. Men who were initially classified as unfit (defined as being in the bottom 20 per cent of fitness levels for a given age), but who—via increasing physical activity—improved their fitness level by the second fitness examination, reduced their mortality rate during the subsequent 5+ years of follow-up by 44 per cent.

Most significant in terms of the weight debate was the fact that the improved longevity prospects were not at all dependent upon weight loss. Results from the ongoing Harvard Alumni Study provide similar results: Sedentary Harvard alums who increased their level of physical activity experienced a 23 per cent reduction in all-cause mortality rate. Because alums who lost weight were no better off healthwise than those who did not lose weight, the reduction in all-cause death rate observed in the more physically active men was in no way attributable to slimming down.

Exaggerated Health Hazards

Despite all this evidence suggesting that lifestyle is far more important than body weight in terms of health, and that it might be more prudent to focus on getting people fit and healthy rather than trying to make them thin, the weight loss industry still barrels along like a runaway freight train. Aside from the cultural obsession with slimness, health professionals have done much to sanctify this quest for a lean body—primarily by fuelling a medical rationale for fat phobia: Obesity is a major killer. The most blatant—but unjustified—example of this scare tactic is the widely publicised claim that obesity kills 300,000 Americans every year. Former U.S. surgeon general C. Everett Koop asserted as much when he launched his Shape Up American campaign in 1994. Since then, this figure has taken on a life of its own, appearing in scientific and medical journals and mentioned repeatedly in the media—each time reminding us of the "fact" that obesity is the second leading cause of preventable death.

The problem, however, is that there is absolutely no way to prove this assertion. In fact, the most frequently cited source of this statistic, a 1993 article in the Journal of the American Medical Association, shows just how misinterpreted this statistic actually is.

The article, titled "Actual Causes of Death in the Untied States," attributes the 300,000 deaths per year to "diet/activity patterns"—not to obesity. Obesity is a physical trait; diet and physical activity are behaviours. To equate them not only is unjustified, it is absurd.

While poor diet and lack of physical activity may lead to obesity, the truth of the matter is that the studies used to generate the 300,000 figure looked at the health impact of poor diet and sedentary lifestyle across the entire weight spectrum, not just among fat persons. (There are a great many less-than-healthy couch potatoes with poor dietary and exercise habits who—via luck of the genes—will never be fat).

2

Path to Fitness

Knowledge is power, and knowing what works is very important. Understanding the factors that contribute to habit formation will provide you with the basics to change your behaviour. However, you must know how to apply this information correctly. Beginners are easily confused while attempting the difficult task of changing their lives. Therefore, below is a priority checklist to help keep you on track:

1. Keep a Journal;
2. Set the goals that you wish to attain;
3. Develop a plan of action;
4. Make a list of habits that you absolutely must change;
5. Note what beliefs that you have associated to these unwanted habits;
6. Carefully define your philosophy of life;
7. Judge whether it is based upon reality;
8. Take small daily steps towards making these changes;
9. Expect set backs and disappointments;
10. Stay focused, learn from your mistakes, and make the needed adjustments;

11. Take it one day at a time—and do not rush;
12. Take on only what you can handle effectively;
13. It takes time and consistent commitment to accomplish your goals;
14. Take detailed notes on your progress; and
15. Visualise your success while practising your new skills. If you take yourself seriously and remain committed, you will make these needed changes.

To help, support your newly acquired lifestyle, these are following suggestions: Find a role model who you wish to emulate, and imitate their lifestyle. Develop a support group to help keep you focussed on your new goals of change; and do not let family or friends sabotage your efforts.

Accurate information will go along way towards reshaping your attitudes and beliefs. However, you must remain consistent and practise your new behaviours.

Clearly, healthy lifestyles require discipline and effort to be successful. Nothing should be left to chance. An excellent example is senior fitness expert Dr. Bob Delmontique. At 78 years of age, he is lean, muscular, and athletic. He is as strong as a 30 year old man, and is in excellent health. His secret for longevity is simple: take an active involvement in your health, get medical checkups, exercise regularly, take nutritional supplements, and develop the psychological and spiritual basis to carry on a balanced lifestyle. He has maintained this outlook since he was fifteen years old, and he intends to continue well past the century mark.

Commitment to health is everything, and wishful thinking means nothing. You must invest personal energy into your new lifestyle. You can't rely on luck to keep you healthy, you must depend on your intellectual resources. You have the power to make these changes—the decision is yours!

Starting Afresh with your workout!

Have you Found yourself Slowly Slipping away from your Health and Fitness Goals?

You're spending your nights, watching TV, wearing those comfy clothes that hide your "back-slidden" training efforts while enjoying packets of chips, chocolates or whatever else you can get your hands on to fulfil the urge to comfort eat.

By the evening the inspiration for which you started the day with has gone, along with the promise you made to yourself that "today was the day" that you were going to restart your fitness programme.

I can hear you sitting there going "oh blah blah blah-I have tried everything and it doesn't work". "I am too tired", "My hours are too long at work" etc.

No doubt you are up to your armpits in reasons and excuses but you can make it happen if you choose you just need to know How to start a-fresh!

Making a Simple Commitment

Now without sounding like you are converting your religious faith or signing your life away make a commitment to your new programme by doing the following:

(a) Taking your measurements

(b) Taking a before photo of yourself

(c) Get yourself a diary that you can keep track of your training and eating with.

(d) Give your new plan a "NAME". This gives you some extra freedom without putting too much pressure on yourself to reach your results within a unrealistic time span.

Your Easy to Follow Plan

One of the biggest mistakes people make when starting a-fresh is starting where they left off. If there is one sure way to shoot your training plans down in flames it's starting with a programme that is too advanced for your current state of fitness.

Sure you could perform this same programme two years ago or even six months ago but remember you haven't participated in any "real" exercise since then and "oh boy" your body doesn't agree to this new harsh form of punishment. You can bet within 14 days your butt, abs, arms, back and anything else that has muscle is going "ouch, ooh, argh, no more"!

To ensure you don't mess things up before you even start giving yourself an honest chance to succeed and start with a routine that is simple to follow that will still offer results without taking over your life.

This could be walking or performing cardio just 3 days per week. Or performing a couple of circuit training classes at home or at the gym every 3 or 4 days, nothing too strenuous just enough to give you some incentive to try a little harder.

Using your calendar mark these workout days with a big tick (not a "x")-a TICK represents something positive!

In your diary write down the exercise that you are to perform and then take note of the exercise you actually carried out. Don't forget to put a encouraging comment next to it-such as "Well done Mandy, 30 minutes of brisk walking. I feel great"... or "Wow, that pump class blew me away! 10/10, great work!"

Don't get me wrong if you want advanced results you need to put in the effort but you can't train using an advanced program unless you've prepared your body for it with some muscle conditioning and of course you need to increase your general fitness. Kinda like performing the backup and preparation work for your training goals.

Starting somewhere is better than nothing at all. And all it takes is a small taste of a few exercise sessions per week to re-kindle your old enthusiasm for training.

Once you've hit the 8 week mark you should be starting to get back into the swing of training regularly. At this point you should upgrade your programme, advancing it slowly, don't over do it, adding another session to your week. Then in another 6-8 weeks upgrade it again.

Obviously it's important at any stage of your programme to seek advise from your doctor and of course be using a programme that is designed by a trainer or a qualified instructor to suit your fitness requirements.

Don't Rush the Eating Plan...

Get started on your exercise routine first, for say a month or even six weeks, then slowly introduce your eating plan. Of course you should attempt to eat sensibly but don't be too harsh on yourself as you are trying to create new lifestyle, none the less one that you've had before, but you still need some balance—rather than turning your life upside down.

You've heard the saying "slow and steady wins the race"—well quite often this is very true and if you're the type of person who doesn't like to be obligated or feels overwhelmed by being over committed then you will find the above steps much easier to follow along with being a whole lot more successful with your training efforts.

How Qigong can Help You Relax Out of Stress

Our birthright is to swim in an ocean of pleasure and harmony, luxuriating in the rolling swell of life. As young children—if we are fortunate—we live that birthright. We celebrate life with a buoyant, carefree, vital engagement in the everyday moment

Then something starts to happen to us. We begin to tense up. We begin to close down. We begin to lose touch with our bodies and live in our heads. We become confused about our feelings. We start to regret the past or fantasise about the future. We begin to fragment. We start to lose our fluid integrity as fully expressed and responsive human beings.

While a certain amount of stress is natural to life, our search for technological shortcuts to comfort and convenience has ironically created unprecedented waves of stress in our modern lives. Our nervous systems are constantly reacting to a barrage of phone calls, faxes, e-mails, frenzied traffic and numbing schedules.

Life seems to have become more of a struggle, with less rather than more time to rest. Sooner or later we really hit the wall. We end up sick in bed. Or a major crisis stuns us into a temporary halt. Stress has got the better of us.

Not surprisingly, the World Health Organisation is now listing stress as a prime contributor to the five leading causes of death— such as cancer and heart disease.

Although most of us are now aware of the dangers of stress, we've become so addicted to the surges and swings of feeling associated with stress, we can no longer imagine life any other way. If things get too quiet we start seeking out a new stressor to react to, for another chemical jolt, another toxic surge of excitement and nervous expenditure.

The Most Effective Self-Care System in the World?

There are many ways to intervene in this vicious cycle and reclaim our peace of mind—restoring balance and serenity in our lives. Meditation, yoga and moderate exercise can all help. But, after twenty-five years of personal research into what works best to counter stress, it is found that the ancient Chinese art of Qigong to offer the surest results.

So Why and How is Qigong so Effective in Managing Stress?

First, qigong emphasises and teaches how to breathe correctly into the lower stomach. When we breathe this way consistently, our lymph systems are effectively activated, detoxifying the body and sending a gentle stream of energising oxygen into the tissues. Activation of the lymph system automatically triggers a relaxation response throughout the body. We automatically feel balanced and "well". Qigong also activates the lymph system with off-the-body stroking movements and an emphasis on pumping the legs with up and down squatting movements.

Secondly, qigong's strong mental emphasis on internal relaxation shifts us out of the sympathetic nervous system (associated with fight-or-flight and our normal reaction to stress) into the parasympathetic nervous system (associated with feelings of pleasure and harmony). This is so important. Overuse of the sympathetic nervous system depletes our adrenals and floods the body with toxic levels of cortisol. We literally burn ourselves out. But like rats hitting the button for more cocaine, we just can't stop. Qigong slowly seduces us back into the gentle world of the parasympathetic and over time we build up a "body-memory" that allows us to choose a different, relaxed response to stress rather than the frazzled, knee-jerk reaction we usually employ.

Thirdly, qigong balances the meridian energy flow in the body, through scientific movement and direction of mental intention. Areas that are depleted are restored to their correct levels; areas that are excessive are "calmed down." As we become more energetically balanced, we are automatically capable of better adjusting to daily stress.

Fourthly, qigong practice builds the skill of becoming tranquil and appreciating the value of that tranquility. Qigong accomplishes this by meditative standing and sitting practices where we go deep inside and use our attention to release ourselves emotionally and psychically. Significant healing occurs at this level of qigong practice, with tremendous implications for stress management.

Lastly, qigong integrates our three major centres or "brains", the third eye area, the heart centre and the stomach. In the computer age, we have become "headier" than ever, losing touch with the wisdom of our hearts and the grounding of our stomachs. Western science and organisations like Heart Math have proved that attention on the heart centre can train the head to process emotions in a less stress-inducing manner. Through its emphasis and cultivation of all three centres, qigong ensures maximum resilience when it comes to handling stress effectively.

Qigong is like a practical course in acceptance and letting go. We learn how to conserve our energy and stay calm, whatever the pressures. We learn how to gain control of our inner being and take responsibility for enhancing the quality of our lives. These are skills you can use and apply for the rest of your life.

Eating for Stress

Any good stress management programme will tell you that all stress is perceived by conscious or sub-conscious mind. It is not an absolute but rather a relative response phenomena to our environment and is best defined by how we "choose" to react. Consequently, stress affects each of us in different ways and to different degrees. The late Dr. Hans Selye, author of "*The Stress of Life*", made it clear that there is no such thing as a stress free life. In fact, no stress equals death, but some stress forms are better for you than others. An example is the contrast between the stress of a well planned 45 minute work-out versus the stress of running to exhaustion in 40 degree weather while being pursued by a Sabre Toothed Tiger. (The latter is not good stress.)

The connection between nutrition and stress can be intriguing because usually wise food choices are the last thing on our mind when we perceive stress. Nutritional deficiencies are rarely the cause of the stress. We do know that our nutritional needs change when we are experiencing stress and we can help the body "cope" with stress by providing enough of the nutrients which are in greater demand or are more difficult to acquire when we perceive stress.

The two most significant issues underlying nutritional problems during stress are:

(a) food selection

(b) digestion.

Food selection tends not to be at its best while we are stressed. We tend to choose "comfort" foods—those easily obtained, easily digested and sweet or flavourful. They give us a temporary but quick lift but are rarely the most nutritious. Poor digestion during stress is the result of the "fight or flight" reaction generated by our response to stress. Digestion is given very little priority by the hierarchy of body functions during these circumstances. This results in fewer digestive enzymes, less HCL acid and poor blood supply to the gut.

The blood finds the brain and muscles to be more important during this period. With poor digestion, even the best food choices will not result in adequate nutrients reaching important body parts like the brain.

If you don't feed the brain, all of your stress management tools will be ignored and you will tend to react at the "stimulus/response" level (a level below rational thought). So you respond with anger, fear, nervousness, sleepless, depression, anxiety, lethargy, etc.

Another major consequence of poor digestion/poor absorption of nutrients, particularly proteins and essential fats is one of self-cannibalism. Your body, in search of protein and fat will proceed to use it own muscle tissue to provide energy for the brain and other vital functions.

This can include deterioration of and muscle tissue including vital organs like liver, heart, kidneys, etc. It is sure that you have witnessed, maybe even experienced, the "wasting away" look of one under severe stress.

They physically deteriorate and the immune system breaks down leading to opportunistic infections (flu, colds, pneumonia, viral invasions) and inflammatory conditions (arthritis, asthma, skin disorders, etc.). Immune deficiencies can lead to heart disease, multiple sclerosis and cancer.

Increased nutrient requirements during stress that are well recognised and considered minimal if you are to help your body to cope with the demands of stress are calories, protein, anti oxidants (vitamins A, C & E) B complex, essential fatty acids, calcium, magnesium and trace minerals. It is also important to understand that when digestion is challenged, even the best conventional food choices may not do the job. An alternative is to choose reputable food supplements, which are complete and known to digest easily.

Calories: Under severe physical stress, such as burns, trauma, fever or surgery requirements increase by 50 per cent or more.

Protein: With the increase in calorie comes a corresponding increase in protein requirements. Part of this is due to the increased secretion of the adrenal hormone cortisol (the bodies natural form of cortisone) which converts protein to carbohydrate to feed the brain.

Anti-oxidants: Vitamins A (or beta carotene), C and E plus selenium are all important in maintaining a healthy immune system. Stress related tissues such as the adrenal and pituitary glands show depletion of anti-oxidants during stress. Consequently, a cycle develops whereby stress depletes the anti-oxidants, which in turn reduces the body's resistance to infection and disease and increases the likelihood of further stress.

The self-perpetuating spiral continues until dietary intervention reverses the cycle. Unless you have been living in a cave, you are also aware of the role of anti-oxidants in the prevention of heart disease and cancer.

B-Vitamins: There are 8 recognized B vitamins which all play a role in the extraction of energy from food and maintenance of the nervous system. Deficiency in these vitamins is considered to be response for the typical stress symptoms of irritability, lethargy and depression.

Calcium and Magnesium: These to minerals go together and are required for every nerve impulse and muscle contraction in the body. Evidence shows an elevated loss of these nutrients during stress. Low calcium accounts for weakened muscles and muscle spasms. Low Magnesium increases the secretion of stress hormones which aggravates the stress responses. Deficiencies in both result in inability to relax and increase sensitivity to noise.

Some Solutions

Try to eat a diet with adequate digestible protein and essential fats. I am a fan to 40 per cent carbohydrate (primarily form vegetable and fruits), 30 per cent high quality protein and 30 per cent high quality fat (not trans fats and low in saturated fat). Make liberal use of high quality protein supplements as snacks, or part of your meals. (A modern solution to modern problems.)

Understand that for good health, supplementation is not an option. Use quality multiple vitamins, anti-oxidants, essential fatty acids (lecithin, GLA, Flax oil, etc.), Calcium and magnesium. Moderate exercise is not only essential for good health but is an excellent way to get a break from stress.

Carbohydrates—Friend or Foe?

Carbohydrates is the name given to one of the three macro nutrients. Fats and proteins are the other two. Carbohydrates are derived primarily from plants (milk sugar lactose is the exception) and best known for their contribution to available quick energy.

Sugars, starches and fibre are the three types of carbohydrates we eat. Sugars in the form of honey, syrups and refined products are well known sources of energy and taste in our food chain. Starches come primarily from root vegetables, cereal grains, corn, and rice. Fibres are the non-digestible forms which comes from fruits, vegetables and grains. Fibres do not contribute to the calorie count but do make a major contribution to maintaining a clean and healthy intestinal system. Most of the carbohydrate sources, fruits, vegetables and grains also carry significant nutrients necessary for optimum health.

So how much do we need? There is a wide divergence of opinion on this. Government agencies and Dietician Associations recommend 55 to 65 per cent of our calories come from carbohydrates. "High protein" diet advocates push for the minimal number of carbohydrate calories. I am an advocate of the 40-30-30 eating plan, where only 40 per cent of calories come from carbohydrates. The remaining calories are equally divided between protein and "good" fat. The modern trend as evidenced by the Canada Food Guide recommends 6-12 servings of grain products and 5-9 servings of vegetables and fruit but only 4-6 servings of protein rich foods.

Many people increase the intake of whole grain products in the form of muffins, breads, cereals, and bagels to increase their fibre intake. You need to know that the average serving of vegetables and many fruits, particularly apples and berries, contain 30 to 60 per cent more fibre than the average serving of grain products. It is interesting that a 1998 book published by the American Dietetic Association lists the functions of sugars (the end product of carbohydrate digestion) as contributing to taste, aroma, texture, colour and body of foods. "All of which add to our enjoyment". Sugar is also listed as a food preservative. There is no mention of "nutritional value", mainly because there is very little value other than as a source of easily obtained energy. The Inuit population survived for centuries without eating carbohydrates and there is no RDI (Recommended Daily Intake) for carbohydrates.

It is increasingly recognised that chronically elevated levels of insulin in the blood are responsible for increased fat storage and may be implicated in creating insulin resistance which is a precursor to Type II Diabetes. Statistics from the World Health Organisation show us that obesity is doubling every 5 years and we now find a new Type II Diabetic every 8.5 minutes in this country and that is a 3 fold increase over the last 5 years. Many blame these two epidemics on chronically elevated insulin levels which occur from living and eating in "Carbohydrate Hell".

Not all carbohydrates are created equal. The refined and the starchy carbohydrates are digested into sugars and absorbed much faster than their higher fibre, less processed, more complex cousins. The measure is known as the Glycemic Index (GI) which reflects the relative rate of blood sugar elevation. This in turn affects the levels of insulin in the blood. Sugar has a GI of 100 and the GI of white bread is 97, which means 97 per cent of sugar. On the other hand nuts have a GI of 15, which means the rate of sugar rise is only 15 per cent.

Obviously to control insulin one should choose low GI high fibre foods like apples at 59 and broccoli at 23, instead of high GI, low fibre bananas at 82 and raisins at 91.

Carbohydrates are valuable sources of energy and other nutrients. But they need to be consumed in combination with proteins and fats to control the rate of blood sugar rise, which controls insulin. This will help to control hypoglycemia, weight gain and the development of insulin resistance.

Try to become familiar with the GI of the foods you eat.

To Drink or Not to Drink?

In the ideal world, we would eat everything organic, like it was less than 100 years ago. However, in this less than ideal world, at least from a nutritional view point, we find food processors, manufacturers and purveyors determined to impress their investors with great "bottom line" profits through whatever means our free enterprise system allows. Unfortunately, nutritional consideration are not first in the priority lists of most Fortune 500 companies involved in the manufacture, distribution and sale of food products.

There are over 6,000 web pages, according to Aspartame Truth Information web site, devoted to discussing, revealing, berating and defending this non-nutritive item which has infiltrated a huge segment of the food market.

The desire to reduce the calorie content of our meals, in order to manage weight, and the wish by those on sugar restricted diets (primarily Diabetics) to enjoy the taste of sweet, are the two driving forces in this market.

Here a phrase "non-nutritive" is used because artificial sweeteners provide no nutrition to our diets nor is the taste of sweet a fundamental necessity for optimal health. All tastes are acquired and for those with a "sweet tooth" will find that if they increase the protein consumption in their diets, the "sweet tooth" will become much less powerful.

Aspartame is the artificial combining of two naturally occurring amino acids—phenylalanine and Aspartic acid. Questioning the efficacy and safety of this product is the subject of the majority of the 6,000 web sites.

One of the reasons for using aspartame is the quest to reduce calories and therefore lose or maintain body weight. However, there is some evidence, disputed by the manufacturers of course, that the sweet sensation provided by artificial sweeteners, including aspartame, can through a "neural/humoral" connection cause the pancreas to secrete insulin regardless of the blood sugar levels. Insulin is the storage hormone and inhibits fat mobilisation, thus defeating the original goal to lose fat. With elevated insulin, which does not combine with blood sugars, you get an increase in appetite and a craving for carbohydrates. This has been reported by several researchers and of course denied by the research of the manufacturing companies.

The other major criticism is that the Phenylalanine component degrades into methanol, which quickly converts into formaldehyde and accumulates in cells. Accumulated formaldehyde can become toxic to nerve cells over time. The industry claims that the methanol levels in question are well within safe limits and recognised by the FDA in the US and the Health Protection Branch in Canada.

The literature reports a myriad of health problems ranging from behavioural and neurological disorders to immune system breakdowns leading to cancer, arthritis, MS, parkinsons disease, ALS and Alzheimers disease. Others report headaches, epileptic seizures, allergies and mood swings. All such allegations are denied by the industry as they report their research.

Independent research finds problems with aspartame research. An analysis of 164 peer reviewed medical studies by Dr. Ralph Walton of Northeastern Ohio University found that of the 90 non-industries sponsored (independent) studies, 83 (92 per cent) identified one or more problems with aspartame. Of the 74-aspartame industry sponsored studies all (100 per cent) claimed that no problems were found with aspartame. Little comfort for the consumer.

Water for Health and Performance

Nearly all the bio-chemical reactions that occur in body cells depend on water and electrolyte (sodium, potassium, calcium, chloride, phosphorous, magnesium, etc.) balance. These balances are not only vital to maintaining life but also affect physical and mental performance.

Water is the most abundant component of the body (60 per cent + by weight). It is believed that it was Mike Colgan of the Colgan Institute who referred to the body as a "Hairy protein bag full of water". This bag of water has many holes which allow for leakage. These holes include skin pores which allow for perspiration (skin leakage) the kidney/bladder system which expels wastes carried by water and the respiratory system which must be moist or breathing would be very dry and painful. Adequate hydration is very important in the maintenance of body temperature. When muscles contract they generate heat which must be dissipated from the core to the body surface and adequate water to maintain adequate blood volume is vital.

Blood, kidney, heart and lungs are made of 80 per cent or more water. Muscle, spleen, brain, intestines, and skin are 72-75 per cent water. Even bones are 22 per cent and fat tissue is 10 per cent water. On a normal, moderate temperature, inactive day you would lose 1.5 litres (6 glasses) of water through kidney filtration (urine production) and another 0.750-1 litre (3-4 glasses) through the skin and respiration. So an average person needs 8-9 glasses per day just to replace average losses. It is true you get some of that from fruits, vegetable, other beverages and food. My "rule of thumb" for water requirements has long been—weight in kgs./2 = gm of water/day. Caffeinated, alcoholic and many carbonated beverages have a diuretic effect and actually increase the daily fluid requirements. One should choose pure water or high quality sport beverage in some circumstances.

Naturally, daily fluid requirements will vary with environmental conditions, clothing and exercise intensity and duration.

Even mild dehydration—1 per cent of body-which would represent approximately.75 to 1 litre of water (1 per cent of 75 Kg = 750 ml.) can create a reduction in muscle performance and start to show dehydration symptoms. Early symptoms are headaches, dry eyes (ask any contact lens wearer what happens after a couple of glasses of wine), drowsiness, loss of concentration, irritability. If the dehydration is 2-3 per cent, serious performance inhibition occurs. Dr. David Costill demonstrated that at these low levels of dehydration 1-3 per cent even the time for 1500 metres was inhibited. The time for a competitive 10 K was reduced by 2.5 minutes which is serious in a 30 min 10 K. Muscle cramps are also a sign of inadequate fluid replacement and electrolyte loss, particularly calcium and magnesium. Even "Lactate threshold"—an indicator of maximal work performance ability is lowered which is not a good thing in high intensity, endurance competition. Thicker blood, fast heart rate, negative changes in blood pressure are other symptoms.

Don't wait until you are thirsty to decide to drink. Fluid replacement is part of a daily plan. Thirst is a sign—too late—of dehydration, performance is already impaired.

You actually lose significant fluid just sitting in an air conditioned car or office. Frequent drinks of water during a long automobile trip will reduce apparent road fatigue. The same applies to sitting at your desk. A friend has a water bottle holder mounted on the dash of car to encourage convenient hydration while driving.

Here are typical water losses during exercise: 1 hour of weight training = 227 gm; 45 minutes of swimming = 283.75 gm, a softball game = 454 gm; 5 mile run = 681 gm, 45 minutes of full court basketball = 681 gm; bicycling for 1 hour = 936.37 gm. and a marathon = 3291.5 gm.

As the environmental temperature, exercise intensity and or duration increases, you need to drink more and may want to switch to a quality sport drink (one made with a glucose polymer like maltodextrin rather than table sugar and 6-8 electrolytes rather than just sodium and potassium) to avoid a condition known as Hyponatremia or water intoxication caused by electrolyte loss and excess water intake. During the famous Daedalus man powered flight over the Aegean Sea (energy equivalent of 3 non-stop marathons) in 1988, the athlete lost only 1.5 Kg and had normal blood chemistry at the end. He drank a cup of high quality sport drink every 15 minutes for just over 4 hours. Cool beverages are absorbed better than room temperature or warm beverages.

3

Being Fit and Young

"Use it or lose it; just do it; just say no; if you have your health, you have everything." Sound familiar? Statements like these have become part of American vocabulary. Not a day goes by that we don't hear or talk or read about the latest way to lose weight, reduce stress, and improve ourselves in some way. We are exhorted to be strong, exercise our willpower and our bodies, avoid harmful substances, fling ourselves into the social arena, and be all we can be.

Our society seems to have turned itself onto the idea that we can and should make a difference in our personal health and well-being. In India and developing countries, the leading causes of death and disability are due to the changing lifestyle practices. Although the extent to which illness or death could be prevented by altering our lifestyle is debatable, it is clear that the choices we make every day influence not only how we live, but also how long we live.

While many people have begun to take action to improve their own health, the majority remains on the sidelines; and it is easy to understand why. The slogans sound good, but putting them into practice is another matter. Many people view problems like heart disease, high blood pressure, and diabetes as things, which happen only to someone else or to older people.

"What's it got to do with me?" and "what could I do about it anyway?" they may ask. The barrage of conflicting messages about what is good for us and what is bad overwhelms some people.

How can we know the experts to believe and where can we obtain accurate and reliable information? Often people would like to develop healthier habits, but just do not know where to start.

Chances are you've had similar thoughts or concerns yourself. How healthy are you? What are the greatest threats to your health? What difference might it make if today you began to change your lifestyle in certain ways?

These questions are common, but you are a unique individual and you must find the answers which are right for you. Rather than telling you "just do it" or because everyone else is doing it, I want to share with you the scientific reasons for asserting a certain lifestyle now referred to as wellness.

Wellness is the active process of becoming aware of and making choices to create a healthier life in all of life's dimensions.

Wellness describes a lifestyle in which the physical, social, intellectual, psychological, spiritual, and environmental components of health are integrated.

The person committed to wellness is continuously striving to achieve the optimum level of health within the framework of his or her own limitations and potential.

The well person takes an honest look at his or her own capabilities and limitations and attempts to change those negative factors in life that are within the individual's power to change. Wellness behaviours include:

- Exercising aerobically at least three times per week and engaging in other forms of exercise daily
- Not smoking
- Limiting the consumption of alcohol to no more than two drinks per day and seven drinks per week
- Taking actions to preserve the environment
- Eating wholesome, nutritional foods
- Reducing caffeine intake
- Practising safe sex
- Engaging in practices of meditation or reflection which enable you to reduce stress
- Consciously avoiding inappropriately hostile or aggressive behaviours
- Avoiding inappropriately passive behaviours
- Balancing work, social, and fitness behaviours

Our outlook on life, our relationships with others, our general appreciation of the world around us, and our respect for the well-being of others are all major elements of the wellness lifestyle. Thus, wellness is not dependent upon age, sex, or intelligence but a mindset which will help you attain a sense of well-being.

Just as certain influences predispose us toward various behaviours or make it more difficult to change a given behaviour; reinforcing factors serve to help us to maintain our motivation to change. Without them we slide backward toward negative wellness behaviours.

Having a strong social support group to give you positive feedback, having a friend to call when you're craving that cigarette or rich dessert and knowing others really and actually care about you may actually help you to continue your diet and exercise efforts. The extent to which you perceive yourself as feeling better and the feedback you receive from others following an adoption to a given behaviour may encourage or discourage your continuation of the behaviour.

While some people participate in a 10 km. race for the T-shirt they get for entering the race, others participate because they feel good about the value they place on the exercise and finishing the race is their true reward. Ask yourself, "What did I do for myself today, yesterday, and what about tomorrow?" Begin a wellness approach by:

- setting realistic goals
- adjust priorities
- identify your resources
- develop a plan and time frame
- take action and give yourself time to make the behavioural change.

Weight Loss and Enjoyment

This holiday or festival seasons don't be trendy–avoid the Seasonal trend. (the average weight most Americans gain between Thanksgiving and New Year's and Indians in festival like Diwali and marriage ceremonies). That's one trend you don't want to participate in!

I know what you are thinking–the holidays are a time for fun and indulgence. You don't want to think about fitness during that time. You want to enjoy yourself. Don't worry! The festivities don't have to be eliminated or avoided. You can have a fabulous time while also maintaining your weight and your fitness regimen.

The secret to achieving a holiday season that is both full of fun and also includes fitness is found in moderation. There are two typical approaches to the seasonal festivities:

(1) throw all healthy habits out the window and indulge in every guilty pleasure;

(2) starve and binge approach (for example, you eat nothing all day long to allow yourself to overindulge in party

food). Of course, neither approach is successful at maintaining a healthy, fit lifestyle throughout the holiday season.

As mentioned above, the key is found in moderation. With a moderate approach both to what you eat (or don't eat) and how much exercise you do (or don't do), you can avoid packing on extra weight and also partake in all the fun of the season. So this season, get a head start instead of starting later, with extra kgs to lose.

Here are some tips to help you:

Create a Plan Ahead of Time: Before the festival and marriage ceremonies sneak up on you, create a plan for incorporating fitness and good nutrition into your daily routine. Evaluate your party schedule and then determine how much time you will realistically have available to devote to working out and/or eating healthy meals.

Don't Put Your Fitness Goals on Hold Until the Season Come: If you can't exercise as often during this time period as you normally do, adjust appropriately. Don't use the excuse that since you don't have time for your full workout you just won't workout at all. Instead accept your limited availability and simply reduce the frequency and/or duration of your exercise. It's much better to cut your fitness time in half than to completely eliminate it.

On the Day of a Party, be Sure to Eat Regularly all Day Long: If the party is in the evening, eat breakfast, lunch and a snack before hand (just as you would on any other day). Once you are at the party, go ahead and indulge in some of the fun, delicious foods. Since you have eaten meals earlier in the day, you probably will find that you aren't tempted to go overboard and eat everything in sight. However, if you starve all day long attempting to save up all your calories for the party, you will be so famished by the time it begins that it will be difficult not to c ereat.

Schedule your Work-outs: Mark them on the calendar and set-aside time to complete them. Consider them as important as any other appointment or event you have marked on your calendar.

When at a Party, Start by Eating Some of the Healthy Offerings: For example, vegetable sticks (without dip), fruit pieces, plain chicken pieces, etc. Then move on to some of the less healthy (but yummy) offerings.

You will be less likely to overindulge on these foods if you have already filled-up on some of the healthier items. Yet, you will not feel deprived or unsatisfied.

***On Fays that You Really Lack Motivation or Simply do not have Time for your Complete Exercise Routine, Commit to do Just 10 Minutes of Exercise*:** You'll probably end up doing more than that once you get started. Even if you only end up completing 10 minutes, that is still a lot better than zero minutes.

When presented with a large variety of food options, it's tempting to want to eat everything. Rather than eating one large slice of chocolate cake or a huge plate of meatballs, select a sampling of bite size pieces of several of the desert or appetizer offerings. This way you get the enjoyment of trying many different foods without overeating.

Exercise at Home: You'll be more inclined to follow-through on your exercise commitment if you don't have to drive somewhere to do your workout. Plus, you won't waste any time on driving, parking, the locker room or waiting to use equipment.

Working out at home requires very little equipment (even can be equipment-free) and is quite inexpensive.

Avoid Wasting Calories on Alcoholic Beverages: The average alcoholic drink contains 150-200 calories per glass.

Indulge in just 2-3 drinks and you've drunk the equivalent calories of an entire meal. If you partake in these beverages, choose wisely.

For example, instead of having a full glass of wine, try mixing half a glass of wine with sparkling water or with a diet cola. This will help cut your calories in half.

***When Running Errands or Shopping, be Sure to Pack some Healthy Snacks to have On-hand*:** Then after you work-up a big appetite, you won't be tempted to grab something at the mall food court or the fast food restaurant on the way home.

Hopefully these tips will help you find a balance between staying fit and also enjoying the fun of the season. Remember, moderation is the key.

Healthy Eating

For many people, holidays, festivals and family get togethers are a time for celebration. These celebrations often involve foods that are high in fat, sugar and calories and short on nutrition. With a few minor changes, however, special occasion foods can be both delicious and nutritious.

Dairy Products...

Many holiday foods include dairy products. Enjoy these foods during your celebrations, but use skimmed milk and other 'low' or 'no' fat dairy products in your recipes whenever possible. Look for the growing assortment of low fat cheeses, cheese slices and cheese spreads that are now available in your grocery store.

For example, use light or ultra-light cream cheese or cheddar cheese with only 7 per cent fat. If you use spreads or other products that are high in fat, such as butter, mayonnaise, sour cream, spread them very thinly or use only a small amount.

The Meat Dish...

Choose leaner cuts of meat for your holiday gatherings whenever possible. Turkey is one of the leanest types of meat. As a general rule, white meat is leaner than dark meat—so choose the breast meat of a chicken or turkey rather than the drumstick.

Trim the visible fat off of meats. Remove skin from poultry. Choose fish more often. Cold-water fatty fish such as tuna and salmon have 'heart healthy' types of fat in them. Prepare meats in ways that reduce the fat content, like broiling, stewing, or baking. Drain the excess fat off of meats after cooking. Cook meats on a rack so fat can drip away. Cool soups, gravies, stews, etc. before serving and then remove the hardened fat that has collected at the top. Use vegetable cooking sprays to prevent foods from sticking. When preparing a roast, baste with low fat broth instead of the drippings from the pan.

Vegetables...

Fortunately, most vegetables contain little or no fat. It is what we add to the vegetables that increase their fat content.

Avoid smothering your vegetables with thick creamy sauces or butter. Potatoes, for example, contain no fat. They also contain very little salt and are good sources of Vitamins B and C and potassium. Potato skins are a good source of fibre (fibre may help lower cholesterol levels, and reduce the risk of colon cancer). Try leaving the skins on the potatoes when you mash them. When mashing potatoes, rather than adding butter or sour cream, try whipping the potatoes with skim or 1 per cent milk or low/no fat sour cream or yogurt.

Feel free to include two or three vegetables with your meal as long as they have been prepared with little or no fat. This can often be done by steaming, baking or cooking them in the microwave. Flavour can be added by using seasonings such as spices and herbs. Dark green vegetables (such as broccoli) and bright orange vegetables (such as carrots and sweet potatoes) are high in the antioxidant vitamins, folic acid and fibre. Antioxidants (as Vitamins A, C, and E) can be protective agents against heart disease and cancer. Folic acid may play a role in helping to reduce the risk of heart attacks and stroke. When choosing vegetables, pick the ones that are the darkest in colour to ensure maximum nutrition.

Salads are a great addition to any meal. Be sure to choose a low fat dressing or ask your host to let you add your own so that you can control the amount.

Cooking Tip: To prevent loss of flavour and vitamins when cooking vegetables, try steaming vegetables in less water or using a steaming rack. If you do boil vegetables in water, save the water to make gravy.

Stuffing...

If you have stuffing with your meat dish and the recipe calls for meat or giblets, replace half of the meat with dried fruits such as cranberries, raisins or apricots. This turns an everyday recipe into a colourful and seasonal dish.

Cooking Tip: Rather than cooking stuffing inside of poultry or a roast, cook the stuffing in a casserole dish or aluminium foil in the oven. This will reduce the amount of fat in the stuffing considerably.

Gravy...

Making gravy from a low fat broth rather than the drippings from poultry or a roast is a good way to reduce fat. If your gravy recipe calls for milk, make sure to use skim milk.

Cooking Tip: If you choose to use drippings for your gravy, pour or skim the fat off the top of the drippings before using. This can be done easily by letting the drippings get cold and, when the fat has become hard, take it off with a spoon. Or, when the drippings are cool, you can also add ice cubes, to which the fat will stick. Remove the ice cubes before making the gravy.

Cranberry Sauce...

Cranberries are an excellent source of Vitamin C. Unfortunately much of the Vitamin C content is lost in the canning process. Luckily home-made cranberry sauce is easy to prepare and the nutrients are retained. Try using cranberry sauce on your turkey instead of gravy.

Cooking Tip: When making cranberry sauce, add sugar after cooking the cranberries to maintain the tenderness of the skin. You may also want to substitute some artificial sweetener for some of the sugar in your cranberry sauce recipe.

Beverages...

Mulled cider or our lowfat eggnog are a good alternative to high fat eggnog. If you choose to have eggnog, have a smaller amount and dilute it with skim milk or use low fat or fat free eggnog.

Diet carbonated sodas can make a very festive drink when added to your favourite fruit juice—try cranberry or grape juice with soda. Nonalcoholic or de-alcoholised wines are improving all the time and make a great alternative for the holidays.

Beating the Blues

Exercise as an antidote to depression and anxiety is not a new concept. In the 18th century Scotland, doctors in mental hospitals prescribed heavy farm chores as "the best medicine" for their patients and documented marked improvements in mood and behaviour. Now scientists are studying the link between exercise and mood changes at close range and coming up with some fascinating results.

One expert in the field says "exercise is clearly associated with mental-health benefits." And moderate exercisers show lowered blood-pressure levels and a resultant positive mood. The key is moderate exercise, performed a minimum of 30 minutes, three or four times a week. Brisk walking, swimming, lifting weights, and bicycling—all achieve good results.

People who exercise regularly, even at something as simple as walking or bicycling, are more flexible. They experience less stress on the muscles and joints when they do bend down the wrong way. Conditioned muscles recover faster, too.

The big problem we all face these days is living a stressful life. All families seem to be too busy to sit down together and share the joys and pleasures of life. The little things that once mattered are no longer important and now there is a race for more money, more time and more material possessions.

By using simple relaxation techniques, exercising and making changes in our lifestyles, we can manage stress and take control of your lives! Once you have become aware of stress, it's time to relax! There are many techniques for relaxing (and no one method is better than another), but the most basic is deep breathing.

One of the body's automatic reactions to stress is rapid, shallow breathing. Breathing slowly and deeply is one of the ways you can "turn off" your stress reaction and "turn on" your relaxation response.

Still another relaxation technique that can help you reduce stress is "clearing your mind." Since your stress response is a physical and emotional interaction, giving yourself a mental "break" can help relax your body as well. When you clear your mind, you try to concentrate on one pleasant thought, work, or image and let the rest of your worries slip away.

A short and quiet walk can do wonders and just a walk around the block will clear your head and often give you a new spurt of energy.

Muscle and joint aches and pains are a common complaint for many of us, living as we do in a sedentary, high-stress society. The cliche warning us to "use it or lose it" isn't far off the mark. Our bodies pay the price for long hours slumped at our desks or nestled in a soft chair watching television. And if you think some of our aches and pains are just another consequence of aging, you're wrong—more often, it's a result of inactivity and weaker muscles.

Doctors now say that walking is one of the best exercises. It helps the total circulation of blood throughout the body, and thus has a direct effect on your overall feeling of health. There are things such a aerobics, jogging, swimming and many other exercises which will benefit a person both physically and mentally. Researchers agree that exercise helps to ease anxiety and lift spirits.

Steps to Help you Avoid Losing the Thrill

What's your excuse for not making it to the gym on a consistent basis? Locker room too smelly? Eye candy not sweet enough? Music volume making your ears bleed? Feeling intimidated by buff bodies crowding the free-weight area?

Most people start off strong with an exercise programme, and then within a few weeks they've got an excuse for not being there. The majority of people will stop participating in a new workout programme within the first 90 days which is why health clubs that are packed in January can seem virtually empty by March.

Which brings us to you.

If you're starting a new exercise programme, you're probably very excited about it, which is great. But that excitement is going to wear off, at which point you'll begin to notice how much time and effort a workout plan really requires.

And that's the point where you may be tempted to start pulling back, or even to quit entirely. But we're not about to let that happen. Follow these steps from the very beginning, and you'll be one of those dedicated gym members who really get their money's worth.

1. *Make Workouts a Key Part of Your Schedule:* Many people see exercise merely as recreation, not a necessity, which means it's the first thing to go when daily schedules get crunched. You need to decide that working out is as important as anything in your life, even as important as life itself.

   If you don't, as soon as the initial excitement of a new programme is over, everything else will get in the way; business appointments, family obligations, TV, sitting on your duff. Write your work-out times into your calendar and stick to them just as you would a vital business meeting.

2. *Keep it Mellow:* You're a lot more likely to keep your programme for the long-term if you avoid letting going to the gym become a hassle. Choose a gym you can get to in a reasonable amount of time at the time of day you're going to train.

   If you're fighting gym traffic, you'll be a lot less motivated. Find a place where you won't have to line up to use the equipment you want. And unless you'll be going at the end of the day and can wash up at home, make sure it has clean showers and a comfortable changing environment.

3. *Don't Bite off More than You can Chew:* Many people often start out too aggressively, going to a level that's higher than they're capable of. As a result, they injure their muscle fibres, so for 48 hours they're walking around like a mummy. Then they stop going to the gym because they find themselves dreading the pain.

Many people don't realise that long, drawn out workouts is Not better. You're not giving your body enough time to recover between workouts. 60 minutes tops (if you're doing a strength and aerobic work-out), or about 30 minutes of a strength or aerobic work-out. Make those minutes count! You can still work-out daily as long as you keep your work-outs short.

4. *Set Achievable Goals:* It's inevitable that as you start a new programme, you picture yourself looking like the models on TV or in the magazines. But if you set your sights too high, you may find yourself discounting the gains you are making. When you're starting out, go over your long-term goals with a trainer or coach, and decide what you can achieve based on your work-out schedule.

   Then, instead of looking far into the future, give yourself intermediate weekly and monthly goals, such as doing an extra rep or lifting 5 more kgs. If you always have new goals to shoot for, it stays interesting.

   Remember: You're not exercising to lose weight. You're exercising because of how you'll feel as a result of exercising regularly. You will get leaner, you will have more energy, you will have a higher self-esteem. If you don't achieve the goals in the time you first set, it's not the goal that's wrong. It's the time frame that was wrong. Keep focused on your goals.

5. *Chart your Progress:* Gains from one work-out to the next can be subtle, and the only way to know how well you're really doing is to write everything down. Keep a journal of your work-outs, as well as what you eat. Even people who are diligent don't remember exactly how well things went if they keep everything in their head.

   When you write it down, you can compare results, see what is and isn't working, and see that as time goes on you're really making progress.

6. *Mix it up:* Doing the same workout over and over again gets old fast, and your results won't be as good as if you try a variety of exercises. Instead of doing 40 minutes daily on the treadmill, try every darn aerobic machine in the gym and go on hiking, in-line skating and bicycling adventures whenever you get a chance.

   Change your weight training routine regularly to keep things interesting and to help break through plateaus. A lack of variety leads to staleness. A good rule of thumb is to change your sets, reps, weight, and rest periods every 3-4 weeks. You'll have more fun if you learn new tools and keep doing different things.

7. *Go One on One:* One reason working out can seem less enjoyable than playing sports is that it lacks interplay with others. But there are lots of ways to have some spirited competition in the gym, whether it's racing >> on treadmills or competing (safely) with your weightlifting buddy. When two guys are on the same regimen, they can make things more fun by having "mini-contests."

   Try going as many reps as you can on a certain weight. Or see who can lift the most weight for 4-5 reps. Just make sure the contest rules specify doing the exercise right, since sacrificing form to lift more weight can be dangerous.

8. *Work with a Trainer or Coach:* Workouts seem easier and are more effective with a professional prodding you on; plus, you're more likely to feel obligated to show up (especially if he's going to charge you anyway). When there's someone watching you and keeping an eye on your progress, there's incentive to keep going. If you can't afford to hire a trainer for every work-out, just do it every couple of weeks or once a month and have him/her help you set goals for you to reach in between.

Also, consider getting a training partner—just make sure it's somebody who will show up every time, is dedicated as you are... in other words, a clone of you.

9. Force yourself to hang in there religiously for the first three months. Nothing sustains motivation better than results. However, whether you're a beginner or a competitive body builder, your muscles must be given enough time to adapt to the growth and recovery periods that strength training requires.

   Though you may see some results, like increases in strength, early on, noticeable changes in your physique can take up to three months. (Note: This doesn't mean that everyone will take this long to see results. I've had clients see results in the first couple of weeks; some waited a few months before things fell into place.)

   It also takes that long to establish a rhythm and discipline to your training schedule, but after three months of dedication, you'll be a lot less likely to fall off the training wagon.

10. *As soon as you Miss a Workout, Re-motivate Yourself:* This is the danger zone, the time when most people start giving up. You've missed one work-out, so what's the big deal about skipping another, or all of them? Before you know it, your whole programme could go down the tubes. If you miss a work-out, you miss a work-out. It's over. You can't bring it back. So it makes no sense to beat yourself up about it.

Nutritionist's Tips

Water: Adequate water can actually reverse athrosclerosis (hardening of the arteries due to plaque build-up). It seems that water can actually flush the arteries of plaque.

It also expands blood vessels and makes arteries more elastic, which is essential for healthy hearts.

Most importantly, I believe, is that adequate hydration raises the metabolism and allows for stored fat to be burned more efficiently as well as slowing heart rate, reducing blood pressures and reducing fluid retention.

Drink enough water to make your urine clear and colourless all day. Limit coffee, tea and pop to three cups a day.

Breakfast: Breakfast should include at least four grams of fibre, which in turn reduces cholesterol and fat in the blood. Every 10 grams. of cereal fibre reduces the risk of heart disease and diabetes by 30 per cent.

It also reduces cancer and diabetes risk. Good sources of fibre are cereals, dried beans and lentiles.

It is suggested that adding nuts and seeds to breakfast cereal and to have a whole piece of fruit as well. Whole wheat toast, a bagel or a bran muff is not a good source of fibre.

It's important that one eats breakfast within 30 minutes of waking.

It also reduces the risk of cancers by preventing absorption of carcinogens and reduces cholesterol by preventing its absorption.

It is suggested that breakfast should be the heaviest, while lunch should be a little less, and supper even less than that.

It is told that the body adjusts and hunger won't be an issue at the end of the day.

So, in other words, our bodies become more efficient and burn those calories when we eat a good breakfast.

Vegetables: Choose at least two different vegetables at lunch and at supper. Eat a minimum of one cup of vegetables at each meal then eat the rest of your meal. Rice, potato and corn are starches and are not counted as vegetables.

Meat: Eat a maximum of 100 gm. of meat, pork, chicken or fish a day.

Walking: Walk for 25 minutes every night after supper. The benefits of walking after supper compared to walking before supper are many.

It can lower your blood sugar by 50 per cent, but best of all when one exercises as described above, your body is burning calories the whole time you sleep.

Most people eat little through the day relative to their large meals and evening snacks. This raises the blood sugar really high before sleeping. Higher bedtime sugars directly create extra weight and extra cholesterol and lower anti-oxidants which help prevent cancer.

Walking for 25 minutes after supper raises your metabolism, releases growth hormones which suppress appetite for late night snacks and act as a natural fat burner overnight.

It is said that one can change diet overnight, but allow an average of 3-5 weeks for these changes, as listed above, to impact your metabolism.

Regular Weigh-Ins: He suggests that if one follows the above, they don't need to weigh in weekly. It has been found, that the stress of weigh-ins create a chemical in our brains which actually retains the fat and thus we reach those dreaded plateaus. It is heard in many stories that people who only had five or 10 pounds to lose, but just couldn't do it. Weigh-ins become so stressful that they create these fat-holding chemicals. Now that was an interesting thing for me to hear!

It is suggested, that we should take monthly body measurements as a true picture of how we are doing.

These suggestions are based on certain statistics—People with cancer, diabetes, high cholesterol/heart disease, bowel problems, and those who are overweight, generally have five things in common!

They are:

* Small or no breakfast with adequate fibre.
* Inadequate water consumption.
* Inadequate activity after supper.
* Inadequate daily fibre intake.
* Inadequate daily vegetable intake.

What You Should Know to Design a Safe and Effective Exercise Programme

A complete fitness programme must include aerobic exercise, muscular strength and endurance conditioning, and flexibility exercise. Aerobic exercise does good things for your cardiovascular system and is an important part of weight management. Muscular conditioning can improve strength and posture, reduce the risk of lower back injury, and is also an important component of a weight management programme. Flexibility exercise is needed to maintain joint range of motion and reduce the risk of injury and muscle soreness.

Aerobic Exercise Can be as Simple as Walking

Walking is a weight-bearing aerobic exercise. So are jogging, rope skipping and dance-exercise. Aerobic exercise is an activity that uses large muscle groups in a continuous, rhythmic fashion for sustained periods of time. There are also non-weight-bearing aerobic exercises, such as bicycling, stationary cycling, swimming and rowing.

Comfortable Pace

A very important aspect of your exercise programme is the intensity. You should exercise at a comfortable pace. You can measure your exercise heart rate to check the intensity of your exercising, or you can take the 'talk test.'

To measure your heart rate, take your pulse as soon as you stop exercising. Count your heartbeat for 10 seconds, then multiply that by six to convert it to a one-minute heart rate. If you keep your exercise heart rate within a range of 55 per cent to 80 per cent of an estimated maximum heart rate (220 minus your age), you're doing well. The talk test is easier to accomplish. Just exercise at a pace that allows you to carry on a conversation while you're exercising.

How Often should you Exercise?

Three to four days of aerobic activity is fine for general health maintenance. If you're trying to lose weight, aim for four or more days a week, being sure you take off at least one day a week.

How Long Should you Exercise?

Work up to 20 or more minutes per session for general health maintenance. For weight loss, gradually work up to 45 minutes or longer at low to moderate intensities in a low or no-impact activity.

Strength Conditioning

Pick calisthenics, free weights or machines. Just be sure that your strength training includes exercises for every major muscle group, including the muscles of the arms, chest, back, stomach, hips and legs.

Start with a weight that's comfortable to handle and keep it up for eight repetitions. Gradually add more repetitions until you can complete 12 repetitions. For greater strength conditioning, add more weight and/or more repetitions, in sets of eight to 12, when the exercise becomes easy.

Stretch for Flexibility

Proper stretching involves holding a mild stretch of 10 to 30 seconds while you breathe normally. Always warm up before you stretch. Like strength conditioning, flexibility exercises should include stretching for all the major muscle groups.

One Last Thing to Remember...

Always check with your doctor before beginning any exercise programme, especially if you're over 40, or have cardiovascular risk factors, such as smoking, high blood pressure, high cholesterol, diabetes or a family history of heart disease.

Positive Self-Image

Because thin females and muscular males are seen as the ideal in our society and because we have come to believe that body size and shape are totally under a person's control, most people enter diet and exercise programmes with unrealistic goals and expectations.

If you continually strive to achieve a socially imposed ideal, you will never be free of your insecurities or your self-consciousness. You must truly realise and then learn to accept that we are not all meant to be fashion-model size.

Our body size and structure reflects not only our eating and exercise habits but also our genetics. The role this latter factor plays in determining weight seems to vary greatly between individuals. We are all born with a certain body type inherited from our parents. Although hardly anyone is a pure body type, there are three different applicable categories: ectomorphs, mesomorphs, and endomorphs.

Characteristically, ectomorphs have a light build with slight muscular development. They are usually tall and thin with small frames and narrow hips and shoulders.

Mesomorphs have a husky, muscular build. They often have broad shoulders, and their weight is concentrated in the upper body, making them look compact or stocky.

Endomorphs are characterised by a heavy, rounded build with shoulders usually narrower than their hips. They have a round, soft appearance and are more often overweight or obese.

When we understand and appreciate our bodies, we are able to work with them, not against them. Although many of us are a combination of two body types, we cannot become what we are not. However, everyone can improve their appearance and their health and performance levels by implementing the principles of a safe and effective eating and exercise programme.

Even if you have a genetic predisposition to being overweight, the way you live is what ultimately determines whether you become fat. Genes clearly play a role, but they certainly don't determine what you're going to have for dinner or how often you exercise. Chances are if you're living an unhealthy lifestyle, you'll become fat and unhealthy.

All of us can't be thin. But every single one of us can be healthy. By focusing on what you're eating and how much you're exercising, you'll be able to achieve optimum health and fitness, even though you may not achieve society's ideal of thinness. Accepting yourself does not mean that you're hopeless and that it's okay to do nothing. It means that you feel good and care about yourself, and that you want to be the very best you can be, regardless of your genetics, regardless of society's standards.

To achieve this level of optimum wellness, you must have a positive self-image. This means that your feelings about your body are not influenced by events in your daily life. For many people, life's problems are projected onto their body. "If only I were thinner—or more muscular, I would have made the team, gotten the job, been chosen.... If only I were thinner—or more muscular, I could meet more people, find the right guy/girl, be happy." This self-defeating habit is reinforced by the images we see in advertising; your body becomes an easy target for everything wrong in your life.

When you have a positive self-image, you value and respect your body; you are also more likely to feel good about living a healthy lifestyle.

No matter how much genetics predetermines how you store and lose fat, the body you've been given will still respond positively to being appreciated and treated well. Focusing on fun physical activity and eating healthy foods will help you feel good whatever your size. Developing a healthy, positive image of yourself is the first critical factor in your fitness success. Having a strong sense of self-worth provides the basis for making rational and affirming decisions about your health. Good luck, stay positive, and enjoy all the wonderful benefits of a healthy, active lifestyle!

Bike + Mountains = Excitement and Challenge

Tired of paved roads? Want to go where there aren't any speed limits? If you answered yes, then your vehicle of choice could very well be a mountain bike. Mountain biking has been an exciting challenge to off-road riders. Its inclusion as an event in the 1996 Olympics confirmed what riders already know: Mountain biking is one of the fastest growing sports in the world, both in popularity and participation.

If you've never been on a mountain bike you might wonder what all the fuss is about. Many riders say it's the freedom. After all, destinations are unlimited on these machines built for rough terrain.

Right Equipment

Mountain bikes are sturdier than your average 10-speed or hybrid bicycle so they can withstand rough roads. They have wide tires that grip the trail, and cantilever brakes, similar to those found on a motorcycle.

When purchasing a mountain bike, be sure that it isn't too large. You should always be able to put a foot on the ground to steady yourself. A helmet is a must, and knee and elbow pads are sure-fire scar presenters.

Your Body on a Bike

Riding a bike is one of the best cardiovascular exercises around. Not only does it provide an aerobic workout, but it strengthens the large muscles of the lower body, including the thighs, hips and buttocks, without putting a lot of stress on the joints. The upper body and arms come into play when climbing hills.

Always warm up before you begin your ride. Pedal in a low gear over flat terrain until you begin to sweat or feel warm.

This usually takes about five to 10 minutes. And don't neglect to cool down when you come to the end of your ride. Gradually lowering your heart rate can help prevent the pooling of lactic acid in the muscles. Again, pedal slowly in a low gear.

On the Trail

Practice makes perfect isn't a cliche when it comes to handling a mountain bike. Once you start heading up hills and mountains and over rocks and steep falls, you'll need to rely on your instincts, which, if they don't come naturally, develop through practice. One of the first things to do is to get a feel for how the brakes work. The front brake on a mountain bike usually has more power than the back, and pulling it alone may send you flying over the handlebars. Practice quick stops before you hit the trail so you can feel how your weight may affect how you stop.

Cantilever brakes are stronger than those on other bikes, allowing riders to control factors such as their rate of decline. When descending a hill, lightly squeeze and release the brakes—a technique called feathering—to prevent the wheels from locking.

Change gears as it becomes necessary in order to keep a steady cadence. Use a low gear when you need power, and a high gear when you want speed.

Climbing requires a shift in your weight that will control the tires' grip on the ground. Short, steep hills may require out-of-the-seat pedalling to garner more power. If you try this on a long climb, however, you'll likely tire before you reach the top. Shift your weight forward, off the seat if necessary, to gain the power you need.

Get Pedalling

You can obtain information about trails in your area from your local library or mountain-biking group. The sooner you start pedalling, the sooner you can test your limits—those set by both your body and your mind.

Tae-Bo

What is Tae-Bo?: Tae-Bo, a unique and challenging fitness system, is a martial arts/aerobics hybrid created by Billy Blanks in 1975. Tae-Bo combines Tae Kwon Do, boxing and dance disciplines and puts them together in a challenging programme set to hip-hop music. A typical one-hour class consists of a series of jabs, punches, kicks and steps, choreographed in a series of eight-count combinations.

The name, Tae-Bo, is a combination of other words. "Tae" means "leg" and it relates to the kicks and lower body part of the work-out. "Bo" comes from boxing and the upper body punches that are an integral part of the work-out. Set to the upbeat music, Tae-Bo can be a very satisfying work-out because it engages the entire body.

Who can Participate?: Tae-Bo is for anyone who wants a complete work-out. But more than just exercise calorie and fat-burning exercise Tae-Bo offers a work-out for the entire body. As with any new exercise programme, you should consult your health care provider first before embarking on it.

Tae-Bo can be done at your own rate. As you build strength, you can do more and you can increase your level of physical fitness, Tae-Bo officials say.

Many women are attracted to the programme as a form of strength building. Since Tae-Bo is set to music, it's a lot of fun. You build strength while enjoying yourself. In addition, while Tae-Bo shouldn't be considered a self-defence course, you can learn defensive moves through it because the programme uses imaginary opponents as targets.

How Soon can You See Results?: According to Billy Blanks Enterprises research, some people report feeling a change in their body the very first time they do Tae-Bo and they begin to see results in as little as three Tae-Bo sessions. Others report change over several weeks. Everybody is a little different and individual results vary.

How Often Should I do Tae-Bo?: First, as with any fitness programme, check with your physician to make sure you can start an intense work-out programme. Tae-Bo can be done everyday or a couple of times a week. For maximum benefit, like any other cardiovascular programme, you should consider doing the Tae-Bo at least three times a week, according to Billy Blanks' Enterprises.

Beginners are advised to start slow and build up their endurance. Tae-Bo is challenging and requires use of your entire body. Don't get discouraged if you get tired quickly in the beginning. The entire idea of Tae-Bo is to maximise the benefits by incorporating the entire body into the work-out.

Where Can You Practice Tae-Bo?: Tae-Bo is a trademark of Billy Blanks Enterprises. The routines and music mixes have been designed by Blanks. The Billy Blanks World Training Centre in Sherman Oaks, CA. is the original setting for Tae-Bo classes. But, if you don't happen to live near the studio, you can get started on your Tae-Bo workout in two ways:

- Find an instructor who has completed the Billy Blanks Tae-Bo training course. The training programme has graduated many instructors. Beware of copy-cat programmes, however. There are many "sound-alike" programmes that promise the complete work-out, but the Billy Blanks organisation says there is no substitute for the original Programme.
- Buy a videotape. By watching the tape and following the Tae-Bo routine, you can get the benefits of the whole-body workout in the privacy of your own home.

The Sneakers

If you've tried to buy a pair of athletic shoes recently, you probably realise that the canvas sneakers of the past have been replaced by high-tech, state-of-the-art athletic gear of the present and future. Consumers are faced with so many options that the task of choosing a pair of shoes has become increasingly complicated and confusing, not to mention expensive. By attaining a good working knowledge of athletic footwear, you will be less likely to fall for the latest gimmick or be coerced into spending above your budget.

Required Items

When shopping for athletic shoes, the most important step is deciding what sport you will be using them for. Most sporting goods stores carry a variety of shoes for activities such as running, walking, tennis, basketball and aerobics. Multi-purpose shoes such as cross trainers may be a good alternative for those who want to combine several sports or activities, such as bicycling and weight training, in a single work-out.

Once you have decided on the particular type of shoe you need, it is important to know how to get a good fit. Remember, no matter how popular a shoe is or how good it may look, it won't do you any good if you have blisters after the first week of wearing it.

The Shoes

When purchasing shoes for a specific sport or fitness activity, you must consider your foot type. People with high-arched feet tend to require greater shock absorption than those with average feet.

High-arched (cavus) feet also suffer from lateral instability and are more prone to ankle sprains. Conversely, people with low-arched ("flat") feet require shoes with less cushioning but greater support and heel control.

After considering the type of shoe needed for a particular activity and evaluating your needs based on your foot type, use the following information to ensure you get the best fit:

- Choose an athletic-shoe store or speciality store with a large inventory. They will have a variety of sizes available.
- Try to get fitted for footwear at the end of the day, when foot size is at its maximum. It is not unusual for an individual's foot to increase one-half a shoe size during the course of a single day.
- Allow 1/2 inch, or the width of your index finger, between the end of your longest toe and the end of the shoe. If one foot is larger than the other, buy the larger size.
- The shoe should be as wide as possible across the forefoot without allowing slippage in the heel. If the shoe has variable-width lacing, experiment with the narrow and wide eyelets to achieve a custom fit.

Final Considerations

Athletic shoes no longer require a breaking-in period. However, they will lose their cushioning after three to six months of regular use. It is important to be aware of when your shoes need to be replaced because, if they are no longer absorbing the pounding and jarring action of the sport, you are more likely to sustain knee and ankle injuries.

A final consideration when buying athletic shoes is price. It is possible to spend anywhere from Rs. 500/- for no-name brands to more than Rs. 7500 for Reebok's or Nike's latest technological wonder. Be sure to consider both your budget and your fitness needs before spending a small fortune on shoes.

Finally, though purchasing may be a big investment, it is not a long-term one. If you spend a fortune on the latest style today, a new style will probably replace it tomorrow. It would be more practical, unless you are at a competitive level, to spend a reasonable amount and get the most for your money.

Pilates Primer

Would an exercise technique by any other name still be as effective? Because of trademark restrictions (which have several organisations embroiled in lawsuits with the owners of the term), some studios refer to their Pilates-like technique as 'the method,' or even the phrase the 'p word.'

This squabble over terminology shouldn't keep you from finding a reputable, qualified instructor. Are you wondering what all the fuss over Pilates is about? The word has been tossed around quite a bit lately. Pilates (pronounced Pi-lah-teez), used primarily by dancers for deep body conditioning and injury rehabilitation, is a 70-year-old exercise technique first developed by German immigrant, Joseph Pilates.

Only recently has it migrated from its long-held position at the fringes of traditional fitness methods such as aerobics and weight training. Hollywood has been a key factor in turning the spotlight on Pilates, as numerous models and actresses pay homage to Pilates for their beautifully toned, fit bodies.

Focusing on the Core

The abdominal and back muscles are often collectively referred to as the body's core. Pilates exercises are designed to strengthen this core by developing pelvic stability and abdominal control. In addition, the exercises improve flexibility and joint mobility, and build strength.

How can one exercise technique claim to do so much? The Reformer, a wooden contraption with various cables, pulleys, springs and sliding boards attached, lies at the foundation of Pilates. Primarily using one's own body weight as resistance, participants are put through a series of progressive, range-of-motion exercises.

Despite the appearance of this, and several other equally unusual-looking devices, Pilates exercises are very low impact. Instructors, who typically work one-on-one or with two to three participants, offer reminders to engage the abdominals, the back, the upper leg and buttocks to stabilise the body's core. Exercise sessions are designed according to individual flexibility and strength limitations.

Pilates exercises are not limited to specialised machines, however. In fact, many gyms across the country now offer Pilates floor-work classes. These exercises also stress the stabilisation and strengthening of the back and abdominal muscles.

Connecting with Pilates

The mind/body connection associated with yoga and meditation also plays an integral part in Pilates. Unlike exercise techniques that emphasise numerous repetitions in a single direction, Pilates exercises are performed with very few, but extremely precise, repetitions in several planes of motion.

So, what will all this focus and stabilisation get you? Well, according to its adherents, Pilates can help you develop long, strong muscles, a flat stomach and a strong back, and improve posture.

Of course, these changes are dependent upon other lifestyle factors, such as a well-balanced diet and regular, aerobic exercise. (Though some may claim that Pilates is all you need to develop stamina and endurance as well, an additional cardiovascular component may be advisable.)

An initial Pilates session typically includes a body assessment, which allows the instructor to pinpoint strength and flexibility weak spots. This is the time to become familiar with Pilates' unique breathing patterns, which don't always follow the exhale-on-the-exertion pattern of traditional exercise.

If you're more comfortable exercising at home, there are several Pilates and Pilates-type videos available, including the Fit & Flexible series, and The Method Precision series. Several home versions of the Reformer also are currently available in the market.

Whether you work out at a studio or on your living room floor, Pilates is an excellent way to challenge your muscles, improve flexibility and incorporate the mind/ body element into one effective exercise session.

The Treadmill

The treadmills have been the number-one-ranked home aerobic equipment for the past three years. If you've decided to join the ranks of treadmill owners, there are a number of factors to consider to ensure that you purchase a machine that meets your needs. There are a multitude of treadmills on the market with different prices. You are likely to find that a treadmill's cost directly reflects its quality.

Before you leave your home, measure the space in which you'd like to keep the treadmill. While the average treadmill measures 64 inches long and 28 inches wide, there are machines that fold up to be stored under a bed or in a closet. Drive to the nearest fitness-equipment speciality store where the staff will be knowledgeable and you can choose from a wide variety of machines. Wear a comfortable pair of athletic shoes—the same pair you'll wear as you exercise on the machine at home.

Consider three key elements as you shop: construction, programming features and the warranty.

Construction

First, look at the treadmill's motor size (measured in horsepower) to determine the machine's longevity. Some manufacturers measure horsepower at continuous duty (the motor's ability to function under a load for an extended period of time), others at peak duty. Look for a motor with a minimum 2.0 continuous-duty horsepower, which will accommodate users who weigh more than 82 kg.

Next, examine the treadmill's belt and deck. The belt should be at least two-ply, 17 inches wide and 49 inches long. The board thickness should measure at least an inch.

The deck acts as a cushion for the joints, legs, back and feet. The most sought-after treadmills feature low-impact decks that flex under the user's foot plant to absorb the shock without rebounding to cause additional jarring. This feature is essential for individuals with shin splints and foot and back problems.

A sturdy frame supports the belt and deck system. Treadmills that usually have a steel frame; some treadmills are constructed with aircraft aluminium frames that offer additional flexibility for impact absorption. Aluminium frames don't rust or corrode and are lighter and easier to move.

Programming Features

Lower-priced treadmills offer basic programming for variable speed, time, distance and calories. However, they seldom utilise user information, and the calorie counters aren't very accurate. The quality of the programming features, such as preset programmes that automatically vary the work-out intensity by raising or lowering elevation and increasing or decreasing speed, rises with price.

Heart-rate control programmes are convenient features that consider the user's age and weight and keep the exerciser at an intensity sufficient to achieve maximum fat-burning or cardiovascular benefits.

Other programming options include incline/grade settings. A maximum grade of 10 per cent may challenge beginning exercisers, while experienced exercisers may need a treadmill that reaches a 15 per cent grade.

Warranty

Most manufacturers warranty against manufacturing defects only, not normal wear and tear, and if a user weighs more than the machine's specifications, a warranty may be voided. Many machines come with a lifetime warranty on the frame, while warranties on features and components usually range from 90 days to three years, depending on the machine's quality.

Higher-end machines often come with a one-year in-home labour contract. You can purchase renewable extended warranties that cover everything from parts to labour.

Is the machine loud? Do you like how it looks? Does it offer a smooth ride? Is it easy to operate? Remember, this product will be around for a long, healthy time, so determine what you want and need from it before you begin shopping to prevent a regretful purchase.

In 1996, The Journal of the American Medical Association reported that, based on a study from the Medical College of Wisconsin and Veterans Affairs Medical Centre in Milwaukee, treadmills provide the most efficient way to burn calories when compared to other popular exercise machines. Researchers asked eight male and five female young adults to exercise on six different types of indoor exercise machines, including a cross-country skiing simulator, cycle ergometer, rowing ergometer and stair stepper.

They compared energy expenditure at ratings of perceived exertion (RPE) levels of 11 (fairly light), 13 (somewhat hard) and 15 (hard), and found that subjects who exercised at an RPE of 13 burned approximately 40 per cent more calories per hour on the treadmill as compared to the cycle ergometer, which produced the lowest energy expenditure.

4

Problem of Obesity

When are we going to take action? The World Health Organisation has, over the last 5 years, repeatedly raised the alarm over the rising incidence of obesity and the associated health risks created by this voluminous (pun intended) problem. The incidence of obesity is doubling every 5 years. Even worse is the estimate that up to 20 per cent of school age children are obese—not just over weight.

We blame poor physical activity habits, excess television viewing, too much web surfing, too many video games and junk food addictions along with other poor nutritional habits. All factors play a role. It is called a lifestyle that supports obesity. To change, lifestyles must change.

Obesity represents the storage of excess calories. Excess calories are stored as fat when the food we eat rapidly changes to sugar (or is already sugar), which increases the insulin production by the pancreas.

Insulin is the storage hormone and while insulin is elevated the body will not and cannot metabolise fat. A recent study published in the Lancet medical journal targets "Liquid Candy" (sugared drinks) as the major culprit in these insulin/obesity wars.

The study, conducted on 548 11–12 years old over a 2 year period in schools across Massachusetts found that each sugared drink (included Hawaiian punch, lemonade, Kool-Aid, sweetened ice tea, soft drinks and flavoured waters) increased the BMI (body mass index) by 0.18. If they increased their daily soft drink intake, each extra soda made them 60 per cent more likely to become obese. Fifty-seven per cent increased their intake during the study with a quarter of them drinking 2 or more cans each day.

On a daily basis, the average teenager is getting 15–20 teaspoons (225–300 calories) of added sugar from sugared drinks and this consumption has doubled over the last decade.

Although "Liquid Candy" is not the only culprit it is a big one but through lifestyle choices/changes it is a factor that is within our control.

Problems and Solutions

Overweight and obesity have become common health conditions and their prevalence is increasing globally. The World Health Organisation (WHO) estimates that globally there are crores of people are overweight, about the same number as those whose living conditions and access to food cause them to be underweight.

Many serious health problems are associate with excess weight. Some of the major correlations with obesity, as reported by Aviva *et all* in the Journal of the American Medical Association in October 1999, include:

high blood pressure – 3 times more prevalent,

type II diabetes – 13 to 18 more common among the heaviest individuals,

gall-bladder disease – 21 times more common,

heart disease – 3 to 5 times more prevalent, and

osteo arthritis – 30 times more common.

My personal editorial comment is that "obesity" *per se* causes nothing other than fatigue from carrying dead weight around all day. Obesity is just one of the obvious symptoms of a larger picture of physical inactivity and poor eating habits. These lifestyle issues contribute to the development of the various disease conditions and obesity is usually the result of the same cause.

A very disturbing trend in obesity statistics is the high incidence among children.

The Nov. 27/2000 issue of the Canadian Medical Association Journal shows the rate of obesity among Canadian boys, aged 7 to 13 years, tripled between 1981 and 1996. Girls of the same age group have twice the prevalence over the same time period. In 2000-01 estimates show up to 30 per cent of Canadian children overweight and 12-14 per cent are obese. When you consider the correlations with other health disorders, it should become apparent that our children need help to prevent future health-care disasters.

I have always taken the position that if you are not part of the solution then you are part of the problem. My effort to continue educating about this problem is my attempt to be part of the solution. Parents, teachers, coaches, and all community leaders have a responsibility to contribute to the solutions.

Just as physical fitness, personal grooming and spiritual practises are supported by your lifestyle, so is overweight and obesity. Overweight and obesity are supported by and a reflection of lifestyle. To change, one must change lifestyle—simple as that, but often not so simple.

In the case of children, their lifestyle is set-up and controlled by the parents. Therefore, parents concerned about overweight issues among their children must seriously evaluate the family lifestyle. Family lifestyle not only affects the child today, but establishes the norm for teenage and adult years. Although correlations between "fat kids becoming fat adults" is not strong in the younger years, it becomes very strong if the child is still obese at age 13 and higher according to various health experts.

Excess body fat is a direct arithmetic equation. When you consume more Calories than you burn in physical activity, you will gain weight. There is evidence that children are exercising less and developing some very poor eating habits. Both of these detractors are family lifestyle issues.

Dr. Everett Koop, former Surgeon General of the United States has said "Except for smoking, obesity is now the number one preventable cause of death". Preventable is the operative word here.

When you consider exercise, realise that the simple act of travelling one mile, walking, running or crawling, will burn 75 to 125 Calories depending on your body size. Simply adding one mile per day to current lifestyle activities (approximately 20 minutes walk) can help to control weight by 4 to 5 kg. per year. Therefore 3 miles per day (approximately one hour walk) can control weight by 12 to 15 kg. per year, definitely enough to make a difference.

If you consider some very simple dietary adjustments, the total weight control issue becomes even more manageable. Dr. David Ludwig from Boston Children's Hospital, in a recent study published in Lancet, concluded that "an extra soft drink a day gives a child a 60 per cent greater chance of becoming obese." Instead of drinking milk or water, children tend to drink, or are allowed to drink, sweetened beverages ranging from soft drinks to flavoured water to fruit flavoured crystals to chocolate milk.

Ludwig also says "The average teenager is getting 15–20 teaspoons per day of added sugar from soft drinks alone. Consumption rates among children have doubled in the last decade." These choices, often call "liquid candy", place the child in "double jeopardy".

First, they lack nutrients–they are "empty Calories". Second, sugar drinks and foods raise the blood sugar level rapidly and that leads to elevated blood insulin. Insulin is the "storage" hormone and while insulin is elevated you cannot burn fat. Even in a moderate Calories eating plan, chronically elevated insulin prevents fat mobilisation for energy and encourages fat storage.

When you realise that all tastes are basically acquired you can begin to take steps to introduce better food choices that will become preferred choices. My suggestion is to introduce the changes in progressively small steps.

The most significant guideline for this change will be to understand the need for protein foods in every meal and every snack; no exceptions. If one has a craving for sweets, their diet is likely low in protein.

Choose milk, yogurt (natural–flavoured yogurts usually have 2-3 time more sugar–sugar free usually contain aspartame and that has other problems including stimulating hunger) soya milk, cheese meats, fish, eggs, nuts, seeds, protein supplements as milk shakes, even protein bars (not all bars are created equal–there are several good home recipes for protein bars).

Protein in every meal and snack is designed to control that storage hormone insulin. You can control it even more by eating some of the protein foods first. This slows down the rate of sugar absorption.

Also try to chose low Glycemic Index carbohydrates–whole grain or sprouted grain breads over white flour, apples and berries over bananas and pineapple, colourful vegetables over starchy root vegetables and never eat anything puffed or popped without some protein support. An added benefit of exercise, in addition to the Calorie burning feature is that exercise reduces blood insulin levels and therefore encourages fat burning.

To make these changes real, it should become a family project. Do not expect success if the parents indulge in soda pop, french fries, potato chips and heavy deserts but expect the overweight child to follow different rules. It will not succeed if it is perceived as a "diet".

Diets fail and set up the Yoyo syndrome of weight loss followed by weight gain. This is a "Lifestyle" issue and a serious one. However, if approached with a rational–small step at a time—attitude, nobody will ever feel it is a "deprivation" experience. In fact, it should become a joyful experience because everybody will begin to feel better and have more energy. Make exercise fun and eating and adventure. Here is on eating adventure worth trying as an example:

Power Pancakes: 1 large egg, 1/3 cup large flake rolled oats, 1/4 cup 2 per cent Cottage cheese, 2-3 Tsp Soya Protein Powder, 1 tsp oil and 1/2 tsp baking powder. Mix well and cook like a pancake. For topping instead of heavy sugar syrup try 1/3 cup of plain yogurt blended with 1/2 cup of berries.

Choosing a Bar

The title does not refer to locating a local hot spot but rather to the task of choosing the right nutrition bar to meet your needs at the moment.

Grocery stores, health food stores, direct sellers, fitness and running shoe stores and even convenience stores are all stocking nutrition bars and some make big claims about their alleged value. You need to know that "not all bars are created equal".

Bars: Bars can be divided into three categories based on ingredient characteristics and intended function.

1. *Meal Replacement Bars:* These bars will have a added nutrient deck on the label that includes the vitamins and minerals added. Government regulations require such bars to meet certain Protein, Carbohydrate, Fat, salt and Calorie criteria. Only Meal replacement bars can include a vitamin/mineral deck. They usually include meal replacement instructions that involves eating one for breakfast and one for lunch along with a responsible evening meal and each bar must contain over 250 Calories. Unfortunately, from my perspective, when a meal replacement bar adheres to Government regulations, they contain too many Calories from carbohydrates and can become insulin stimulating disasters which will inhibit fat mobilisation for energy. My recommendation usually suggests the inclusion of more protein when using such a bar.
2. *Snack Bars:* Can really be any bar without a nutrient deck added. As long as the ingredients are generally regarded as safe these bars can be made of any food item with a wide range of Calories, Protein, Carbohydrate and Fat. These include all the "chocolate bars" in the confectionary/candy counters and many so-called sports bars that may be either high carbohydrate or high protein snacks. It is illegal in Canada to "fortify", like they do with cereals, a "snack" bar. My recommendations in this category are to avoid the high carbohydrate sugary snack bar (an exception may occur if you find such a bar palatable during an endurance event that lasts longer than 90 minutes) and choose the higher protein sports bars. Naturally there are "quality" differences ranging from ingredient sources to chemical additives but that would take a long explanation.
3. *Fruit Bars:* These are really just dried fruit pressed into the shape of a bar. The nutritional content will vary with the amount of processing the fruit was exposed to, the

selection of raw materials, the preservatives added and the packaging. If this were your choice you might find dried fruit (without chemicals) a less expensive and more reliable source of nutrients. My recommendations here are to minimise fruit bar use because they contain very little protein and will still contribute to rise in a blood insulin levels and that will lead to fat storage.

Optimal Nutrition

Optimal nutrition for sports and exercise has three major objectives.

1. *Optimal Performance*: Expressed as speed, strength, power and endurance.
2. *Optimal Recovery*: So you can do it again very soon.
3. *Optimal Health*: So you can repeat it forever–well at least for a long long time.

What to eat before, during and after exercise has provided the platform for many "round table" discussions—in the parlour, the classroom, the locker room and your favourite watering hole. Students of ancient history will recall accounts of dietary manipulation for optimal performance going back to the Gladiators. They apparently ate ground lion's teeth and raw meat prior to performances in hopes of acquiring the ferocious characteristics of the lion.

Science and experience have produced many trends and attitude changes over the years and this is a summary of where that has lead.

Before Exercise

Develop a way of eating that will optimise your health. This should include the storage and replacement of adequate energy in muscles so you are always ready for action. I adhere to "The Better Balanced Diet", the 40-30-30 approach. That means 40 per cent of calories from carbohydrates, preferably with a low glycemic index. 30 per cent of calories from good quality, easily digestible protein and 30 per cent of calories from good quality fats. The fats should include approximately equal portions of essential fatty acids, mono unsaturated fats and saturated fats.

My strongest warning is "do not go below 30 per cent of calories from fat", except in the meals 24 hours prior to an endurance event. You make good use of fat during exercise and it has other redeeming qualities (the subject of a future column). This way of eating should ensure adequate muscle glycogen stores for most exercise tasks which last for up to one hour and still provide the nutrients for optimising the immune system and maintaining adequate blood glucose levels to feed the brain.

In anticipation of high intensity and long duration activities, it is wise to top up glycogen stores and blood sugar with a prevent meal higher in carbohydrates (approximately 60 per cent of calories) but do not ignore the protein.

A recent article in the American Journal of Nutrition recommends the protein content of a prevent meal remain at 20 per cent or higher. It has now been well established that endurance athletes demand more protein than weight lifters. After all they challenge their systems at 75 per cent ++ of aerobic capacity for considerably longer times than non-endurance athletes.

It is always wise to ensure adequate hydration prior to commencing activity. In intermittent activities like team sports, individual skill sports and sprint events, water is usually the beverage of choice. Marathons, triathlons and other ultra endurance challenges may warrant the use of a good quality (one with 6 to 8 electrolytes and primarily a glucose polymer carbohydrate source) sport drink of 227 grams to 454 grams in the half hour prior to performance.

During Exercise

Most events lasting less than one hour demand the replacement of lost fluid every 10 to 15 minutes, if optimum performance is the objective. Even small increments of dehydration have shown significant decreases in performance. Short duration events without water will not hurt your health but may not give you optimal performance. Water is usually adequate. Longer duration events and/or within a very hot environment, electrolyte and carbohydrate replacement will be warranted.

The objective of a carbohydrate drink during the performance is to maintain blood glucose levels, to spare the stored protein and glycogen, by providing easy accessible energy for the brain and some of the working muscles. The brain uses glucose for energy so you never want to become hypoglycemic during a performance. If you choose to use one of the "Gel" products you must drink lots of extra water or you will find them counter productive.

Remember, there is no evidence that an overload of carbohydrates in muscles or blood will help performance in sub one hour activities. Muscle glycogen depletion only becomes a limiting factor when the intensity is high (over 75 per cent of aerobic capacity) and the duration is long (over one hour). Similarly, blood sugar cannot exceed certain levels. If blood sugar is chronically high it will induce an insulin response which is reflected by fatigue during exercise.

After Exercise

A long time friend, who holds several weight lifting records, once said to me "The three most important elements of training for optimal results are recovery, recovery and recovery". That is when all of the "good things" happen to your physiology. It is probably the most ignored part of athletes' diet and yet it may be the most important part.

Naturally you want to re-hydrate immediately after heavy exercise. This will help to carry the electrolytes to their proper places, help to cool the system and help to carry accumulated toxins out of the body. Plan on drinking 2 cups for every ½ kg. of sweat lost.

The second objective of recovery is replacing muscle and liver glycogen stores and the replacement of the "branched chain amino acids" (BCAA), the protein portion which is metabolised during exercise. If you don't replace glycogen, recovery of energy is slow and your willingness to do it again soon, is one of reluctance. Plan on consuming 50 to 100 grams of carbohydrates within the first 15 minutes of recovery. Go for liquids first. Following a marathon type of activity, plan to eat approximately 600 grams of carbohydrates within the first 24 hours following the event.

If you don't replace the BCAA's, you find your muscles talking strange languages (stiffness and soreness) to you approximately 1 to 2 days after the intense work-out. To encourage the glycogen replacement, consume adequate and in this case, high glycemic index carbohydrates in the 2 hours immediately following exercise. This is the one window of opportunity when you want insulin to rise quickly and induce storage of glycogen. The elevated insulin will also help to carry the BCAA's (assuming you consumed some) into the muscle. So it is also wise to include some protein in your recovery plan.

Dr. John Ivy published a study in 1992 in the Journal of Applied Physiology which demonstrated optimum glycogen and BCAA recovery occurred when a recovery drink of carbohydrate (glucose polymer) and protein (whey protein isolate) in the ratio of 3:1 in favour of the carbohydrate was consumed. Others have reproduced these results in recent years and it has lead to the development of some excellent recovery drink products.

You could also use cereal in milk or protein powders in juice. The third recovery strategy should be one of optimal nutrition. That means nutrition high in vitamins and minerals. During exercise, we naturally produce free radicals which are molecules that become toxic when exposed to oxygen. These oxidised free radicals are apparently responsible for many ailments ranging from flu and colds, to cancer and heart disease. It has been shown that 40 per cent of Marathon finishers are ill within one week of finishing their run. That is a sign of a depressed or challenged immune system. The only thing that helps to build and maintain a healthy immune system is adequate nutrition. So eat lots of colourful vegetables, protein, essential fatty acids and take your supplements to stay happy in your exercise.

Nutrition Jargon

We live in the era of the most "formally educated" population in the history of the world. The media, in its massive proliferation of printed, video and audio sight and sound bites, attempts to keep pace with the educated masses, by offering an endless stream of information about an endless stream of topics. Health and fitness is one of the hottest topics today and the information stream often contains jargon which may seem like a foreign language to some.

Do you understand all of the nutrition terms used in the media today? You could use this list of definitions as a self-test and gloat about your results or quietly enjoy the little bit of education it offers.

Free Radicals

Unstable molecules which can be very destructive to human tissue particularly when combined with oxygen. Molecules are stable when they have pairs of electrons around the nucleus. When there is an odd number of electrons, the molecule becomes unstable. This occurs in the presence of cosmic rays which we are all exposed to if we live on Earth, pollution, alcohol, radiation, sunlight, environmental chemicals, heavy metals exposure, physical trauma, emotional stress, rancid fats, cheap oils, and even exercise.

These unstable molecules are known to steal an electron from another molecule and oxygen is a very available target. This theft sets up a chain reaction of electron thefts which is known as oxidation (in fat it is known as lipid peroxidation which is also known as Rancid).

Uncontrolled oxidation leads to cellular damage and becomes the underlying cause of many ailments. Free radical development is a natural process necessary for the control of bacteria, the disposal of toxins and the recycling of our cells. It is the out of control Free Radicals that create the problems and this happens when exposure to the above list is excessive and the nutrition for protection is inadequate.

Antioxidants

These are not somebody's relative but rather nutrients which neutralise the Free Radicals. Therefore they protect the body from some of the ravages of damage. They have been dubbed the "Free Radical Scavengers". They include Vitamins A, C and E, beta carotene, selenium, grape seed extract and riboflavin (a B vitamin). A good reason for eating your fresh fruits and vegetables as they are the biggest suppliers of antioxidants. Most research suggests that it is difficult to get enough of these protectors from a diet, due to calorie limitations and available quality produce. Therefore, responsible supplementation becomes a modern solution to a modern problem.

Trans Fatty Acids

Fatty Acids, which have been heated above 160º F. Occurs in the popular processed food action known as hydrogenation. Fatty acids change their configuration and consequently their behaviour in human metabolism. Some become toxic and behave like Free Radicals, others compete with the good fats—essential fatty acids.

This may upset the production of some of the good "super hormones" which, in turn, are responsible for controlling inflammation and fat metabolism. Some behave like saturated fats leading to increased blood cholesterol and triglyceride levels. The most common sources are most margarine, cheap vegetable oils, and deep fried products. Trans fatty acids are implicated in heart disease, cancer and immune deficiency diseases. Should be avoided at all costs.

Homocysteine

One of the essential amino acids (methionine), a component of complete protein, is used to make homocysteine. This is a building block for other necessary items in the metabolic chain. However high homocysteine levels are considered toxic. Vitamin B-6 deficiencies are the most likely cause of excess build up of homocysteine and this has been implicated in heart disease. In fact, homocysteine levels are now used by many Physicians as red flag indicators to predict heart disease. The best recommendation is to be sure you eat adequate levels of B complex, also known as the stress vitamin.

Folic Acid

This B vitamin is one of the recognised essential nutrients for the development of a normal fetus. It is one of the most recommended supplements during pregnancy. It is best known for encouraging proper cell division in the developing fetus, prevention of Spina Bifida and Neural Tube disorders during pregnancy. Folic acid bio-availability is not easy to achieve and the foods highest in Folic acid are not necessarily main stream. Recent laboratory tests have shown that Folic acid availability in 11 of 14 B complex supplements didn't meet standards necessary for required bio-availability. Folic acid is also implicated in the prevention of colon cancer, heart disease and stroke. This is a nutrient you don't want to be without.

Bio-availability

This is a term used to describe the amount of a nutrient that can be absorbed and used by the cells of the body. Bio-availability is affected by the heat in food processing, the fibre content of a diet, the co-factors present or absent in a food or supplement and the health of your digestive system.

If you knew all of this you can gloat to your friends. Now everybody reading this knows it also, so it could become routine parlour room conversation. Best wishes and good health to all.

Nutrition Adjustment

The winter season and the typical events that occur throughout the winter create significant challenges to the immune system.

When the immune system challenges become excessive it manifests in the form of some type of illness. Illnesses ranging from the common cold and flu to more serious conditions leading to cancer and heart disease.

If you develop and maintain a healthy immune system there is no reason for your body to participate in the so-called flu and cold season. In fact it might be more correct to refer to it as the "weakened immune system season". Please appreciate that the "immune system" is not like any other system (cardiovascular, respiratory or digestive systems) in the body.

You can't see it nor localise it. It is really just a term to express all of the mechanisms your body uses to protect and defend itself from the invasions of bacteria, viruses and toxins from the outside world.

Immune system strength is determined by the food you eat and your responses to the "stresses of life" (the neural-humoral connection). The food you eat provides the building blocks for healthy cells that are the most significant part of healthy immunity. During the "busy-season" and the various celebrations we enjoy, often the food choices and other lifestyle habits are not optimal.

To enjoy a healthful, illness-free, high-energy winter, think about forward planning your food choices so they become part of your lifestyle. Don't let "lifestyle" dictate convenient, less healthful food choices. Appreciate the fact that your current state of health is supported by your lifestyle. To change your health and ill-health risks you must change your lifestyle. "Magic Bullet" products and quick fixes will not endure.

Lifestyle Choice # 1: Eat enough protein to support optimal health and chosen lifestyle activities. You require approximately 0.75 to 1.25 grams of protein per kg of body weight depending on your physical activity level. (I know that is higher than conventional recommendation, but trust me it works.) As many know I advocate an eating plan of 40 per cent carbohydrate, 30 per cent protein and 30 per cent carefully chosen fat.

A caveat is to understand that you only effectively absorb 30 to 35 grams (141.875 gm steak = 35 gms) of protein per meal or snack so it is necessary to distribute your consumption though-out the day. Eat some protein in every meal and every snack. There is recent evidence that (at least in the Western world it is recent) at least 30 grams of your daily protein should come from soy to provide adequate "isoflavanoids to help build and protect the immune system".

Lifestyle Choice # 2: Select low "glycemic index" (GI) carbohydrates and avoid those easy to digest high starch and sugar products. GI is a measure of how fast blood sugar rises after eating—sugar = GI of 100 whereas peanuts = GI of 15.

That means peanuts raise blood sugar at rate of only 15 per cent of that created by white sugar—, lower is better. Fast rising blood sugar means the pancreas produces or over produces insulin.

Spikes in insulin production and chronically elevated insulin weakens the immune system and interferes with the production of the "Super hormones" that control many of our other hormones. If you eat low GI carbohydrates, combined with adequate protein and eat some of the protein first, you will control your insulin and be a friend to your immune system.

Lifestyle Choice # 3: Consume adequate "essential fatty acids" (EFA's) from nuts, seeds, fish, cold pressed oils and supplements. EFA's are the building blocks for the "super hormones". Low fat, and high carbohydrates diets put you at risk.

Lifestyle Choice # 4: Understand that nutritional supplementation is no longer an option if you wish to have optimal health and protect your immune system. On the average we eat less that ½ the Calories that our relatives ate in 1900 (1900 = 3800 Calories, today = 1800 Calories). And much of the food eaten today has a lower nutritional density. Remember that in 1900 "everything" was organic. In addition, modern life has dramatically increased the risks of free radical damage through the chemicals and toxins in our air, water and food supplies.

Numerous reputable research papers and books have demonstrated that the protective levels of the three major anti-oxidant nutrients (beta carotene, vitamin C and vitamin E) are much higher than we can expect to receive from any typical diet. Estimated protective levels of beta-carotene and other carotenoids has been estimated at 50,000 i.u., (30 mg) per day, the equivalent of 6½ average carrots or 5½ sweet potatoes everyday. The suggested protective levels for vitamin C are in excess of 1,000 mgs per day, the equivalent of 15 average oranges everyday, assuming the oranges contained vitamin C–some don't. The suggested protective level for vitamin E is at least 400 i.u., equivalent to 19 cups of almonds or 2.1 cups of soyabean oil. I think these examples demonstrate the difficulty one would have in receiving protective levels of essential anti-oxidants from any average diet. Many other examples of such difficulty are available.

The anti-oxidants mentioned above are merely the most publicised examples available. Other significant anti-oxidants include grape-seed extract, selenium, coenzyme Q 10 to mention a few.

Anti-oxidants are known as "Free-Radical" scavengers. They combine with Free-Radicals to prevent them from being oxidised. Oxidized Free-Radicals are the toxic versions and the ant-oxidants basically neutralise them and allow more available oxygen for energy production. When we exercise we produce more Free-Radicals and breath in more oxygen thus increasing the risk of Free-Radical damage. Surveys have shown that up to 40 per cent of Marathon finishers become ill in the week following completion. It therefore behooves all heavy exercisers to protect themselves by increasing their anti-oxidant consumption.

Many people have used or heard of herbal remedies as protectors from flu and colds. The expression is that herbs like Echinacea "stimulate" or "support" the immune system. This has lead to the use of these products upon the appearance of symptoms. However it must be understood that herbs are "herbal remedies" or "herbal medicines" and not food. Echinacea may well stimulate the immune system but if you don't feed the immune system with protective and constructive nutrients, the effectiveness of herbal remedy will be limited or short lived.

So as the "challenging" season approaches you might consider developing a strategy for a wise and consistent food choices and be wise and responsible supplementation along with other smart lifestyle choices like stress reduction, healthy exercise habits and looking after your spirit and soul.

Proteins

Protein is the Answer.

Protein Makes a Comeback.

Protein Comes First.

Athletes and Elderly Maybe Protein Deficient.

High Protein Diets Applauded.

High Protein Diets Criticised.

High Protein Diets Dangerous

—and the list goes on.

These are actual recent headlines in the popular press. Even the talk show hosts are on the band wagon with interviews about the pros and cons over more protein or less protein in the diet. I thought it appropriate to offer a primer on protein to help the consumer sort out fact from fiction or science from innuendo.

The word Protein comes from the Greek word Protos or Proteose depending on who you read and it means "to come first". It has been recognised from early times to be absolutely essential for life. Protein (made from combinations of 22 known amino acids) makes up our DNA, hormones, enzymes, muscles—including skeletal, heart, smooth muscle which surrounds our arteries, immune cells, liver, kidneys, glands, etc. Some of the amino acids 8 or 9 (depending on who you read again) are considered essential which means we must consume them so we can make the other 13 or 14 amino acids and thus create proteins.

Even primitive man understood the importance of protein foods by following their protein sources. When the fish, fowl or animals became scarce, they moved on. We plan our meals around the protein dish (pasta may be an exception but that doesn't make it right).

Restaurant menus are categorised according to protein source and protein usually commands a significant portion of the grocery budget. The primacy of protein persists. It is preferred because most protein rich foods are tasty, satisfy hunger and are rich in other nutrients.

Protein critics have often stated that North Americans eat too much protein. That protein will contribute to osteoporosis by leaching calcium from the bones. They also refer to potential kidney damage and the dangers of Ketosis which refers to incompletely metabolised fats which occur in some high protein–low carbohydrate diets. Like the Atkins Diet, the Protein Power Diet and the Type II Diabetes Diet.

The Guidelines

According to a symposium published in the Journal of Nutrition, there is no evidence of an increase in calcium excretion when one "self selects" a high protein diet from high protein foods. "This is likely due to the high calcium content of such foods".

On the other hand there is evidence that low protein intakes are associated with negative calcium balance and likely reductions in bone density. Studies which have reported higher calcium excretion during high protein consumption have assumed bone loss but not measured it. In fact it may simply be a case of less calcium absorption of the calcium present in the high protein food. Adequate protein is necessary for optimum bone health. The only studies which have demonstrated kidney problems with high protein diets have used extremely high protein intakes. Levels like 600 grams per day which represents 2400 Calories or 85 per cent of the diet. Nobody would naturally eat this kind of diet because protein controls appetite and it would be very distasteful.

When it come to Ketosis, Dr. Calvin Ezerin, author of the Type II Diabetes Diet and a professor of endocrinology at UCLA, has stated that there is no danger to "dietary induced ketosis". Of course, there may a downside and that is bad breath and body odour from the ketones but they are not dangerous. There are, on the other hand, reports of low protein diets that weaken the immune system, increase the chances of yeast infection, and slow the ability to recover from injury. Dr. William Evans of Penn State University has written that any person who eats only the minimum protein, could find themselves protein deficient after a bout of moderate exercise or during a physically demanding job.

Dr. Vernon Young of MIT University has published research that supports the position that we should be eating two to three times more protein than current recommendations.

The American Journal of Clinical Nutrition recently reported that women who ate 24 per cent or more of their calories from protein experienced significantly fewer heart and cardiovascular problems. In another report from the journal Cancer, it was shown that women on high protein diets experienced better breast cancer survival rates. In the same study, contrary to many previous reports, fat intake (including saturated fat) had no bearing on the results. According to Dr. Boyd Eaton, a specialist in Paleolithic diets, 30 per cent of the primitive diet was protein. This level would be consistent with the recommendations of MIT professor Young.

My take on this is as follows:

— because protein comes first, we need between 0.75 gm and 1.0 gm per ½ kg. of desirable weight.

— eat protein in every meal and every snack and make it 30 per cent of your calories.

— never eat more than 35 grams of protein in a single sitting, that's all you can absorb.

— as physical activity or stress increase our protein requirements increase.

— remember that protein controls appetite, and

— eat some of your protein selection first in every case to control the rate of rise in blood sugar. This will avoid hypo-glycemic reactions and spikes of insulin production.

Protein Supplement Lingo

Have you ever wondered about the jargon used in protein supplement advertising and in popular articles extolling the virtues and pitfalls of various types of protein supplements? The following is an abridged explanation of some commonly used terms which hopefully will make you a more informed consumer.

Soy, Whey, or Egg Protein "Concentrate"

This usually refers to a protein supplement source which has been concentrated through high heat drying (dehydration), acid extraction or filtration to reduce the original source to a more concentrated protein commodity. This is the least expensive method of protein extraction but unfortunately other things like lactose, fat and some impurities are also concentrated with it. It is usually 60-70 per cent protein by dry weight.

Soy or Whey Protein "Isolate"

Isolates are created through an alcohol wash or a water wash or some ionisation concentration techniques. The objective is to separate the carbohydrates and fats from the protein. The water method is the least expensive and the ionisation technique is the most expensive method.

The concentrate or should I say isolate is them filtered to further purify the protein fraction. In the case of soy protein isolates, the alcohol version will be devoid of the now famous "isoflavones" which are the "phytochemicals" on soy responsible for many of the "good" things attributed to soy. Isolates are usually 90-95 per cent protein and the best will be water extracted.

Microfiltration and Cross Microfiltration

These are merely terms to describe the type of filter used to further remove some of the unwanted variables from the concentrated protein. No Magic here—just a process similar to Reverse Osmosis in the water purification industry.

Ion Exchange

All molecules possess negative or positive electrical charges. This method extracts or separates protein molecules from most other fractions in the source by taking advantage of these electrical charges. It is primarily used to create Whey Protein Isolates. Again, No Magic here.

Hydrolysed Protein

Hydrolysed or hydrolyses is a method of adding water to protein molecules to help break (lyses) them into smaller parts called peptides. Peptides are collections of 2 to 5 amino acid (the building blocks of protein) chains which are theoretically absorbed faster. It is something like a form of pre-digestion. Sources indicate that this method is the most expensive approach to concentrating proteins and rarely appears as the first ingredient on a protein supplement label. Some companies will add enough to get it on the label in an attempt to make their product look better.

A second issue is that unless you are very ill (hospitalised and on venous drip) or you have a very challenged digestive system, there will be little benefit to this more expensive version. Rapid absorption might be of value to rapid recovery during a long power lifting competition.

Protein Efficiency Ratio (PER)

An outdated method of evaluating protein quality based on the rate of growth of young rats using various protein combinations. A PER above 2.5 was considered excellent based on Egg and casein (milk protein) with a PER of 3.0. This method gave too much weight to the importance of the essential amino acid Methionine which is more important to developing hair on the rat than it is to human nutrition.

Net Protein Utilisation (NPU)

Another outdated or seldom used measure to reflect the value of protein foods. It is basically the amount of protein that a given food makes available to your body based on digestibility and the amino acid composition. A value of 100 indicates that every of protein eaten would be used to produce lean tissue. The highest NPU is egg protein with a score of 94.

Biological Value (BV)

Also outdated but it is a system which evaluates protein based on the amount of nitrogen retained by the body after absorption of a protein food. Again the egg is the standard and the highest value possible is 100 even though some companies try to tell you different about their products.

Protein Digestibility Corrected Amino Acid Score (PDCAAS)

A mouthful but currently the protein quality system considered to be most reliable. The highest score is 1.0 and this is given to any protein source considered complete for use by the human body. Soy protein isolates, egg white, whey protein isolates and casein proteins supplements all scored 1.0 on this test. Beef scored 0.92 and beans were at 0.68.

5

Losing Weight

I am not advocating that we should be complacent about obesity. It's just that continued focus on weight loss seems counterproductive, and may be quite hazardous to the health of those who continually battle their weight. Each year millions of people attempt to lose weight, shelling out crores of rupees in the process. But despite our perennial efforts to shed kgs, our waistlines are getting bigger, not smaller. It seems what ever we lose, we gain back—and then some. Not only can this be damaging to our self-esteem and mental health, chronic fluctuations in body weight may also do physical harm.

In fact, most of the epidemiological studies on weight loss alone show that weight loss increases risk for premature death, primarily from heart disease. This obviously represents a paradox, because weight loss is thought to improve cardiovascular disease risk factors. But this is not always the case.

One of the most popular weight reducing strategies of the past 35 years, the low-carbohydrate diet, actually raises cholesterol levels (especially low-density lipoprotein cholesterol) and reduces high-density lipoprotein cholesterol (the heart-healthy kind) despite weight loss. This suggests that going on a low-carbohydrate diet may actually increase risk of atherosclerosis.

Another possible explanation for the paradoxical finding of weight loss being associated with increased risk of dying from heart disease is the recent evidence which shows that dieting depletes body reserves of heart-healthy omega-3 fatty acids, thus raising the possibility that weight loss via calorie restriction may actually make the body more vulnerable to atherosclerosis. The researchers who reported these findings warned that "a subtle but chronic risk state could be established if recurrent dieting depletes omega-3 reserves and intake during maintenance does not allow effective repletion."

Metabolic Fitness

We need a new approach to health and fitness—one that places less emphasis on body weight (or body fat) and more emphasis on healthy metabolism—becoming "metabolically" fit. To achieve "metabolic fitness" does not require having a lean body, nor does it depend upon having the cardiovascular system of an endurance athlete.

In scientific/medical terms, metabolic fitness can be defined in terms of how the human body responds to the hormone insulin. "Insulin sensitive" bodies tend to have excellent glucose tolerance, normal blood pressures, and heart-healthy blood lipid profiles. Therefore, insulin sensitive people tend to be at lower risk for type II diabetes and heart disease than people who are "insulin resistant"—a metabolic condition in which the body's cells (mainly those in skeletal muscle, liver and adipose tissue) don't respond normally to this hormone, and which ultimately may result in disordered lipid metabolism and elevated blood pressures.

Insulin resistance is associated with high risk for type II diabetes and heart disease.

Although genes play a role, the major causes of insulin resistance are lack of exercise and consuming a diet high in fat (especially saturated fat) and refined sugar, and low in fibre—a description that fits many peoples. Because these behaviours also promote obesity, the "insulin resistance syndrome" (also known as the "metabolic syndrome") is observed more often in fat people than it is in thin people. But as I have pointed out already, a fat person with the metabolic syndrome does not have to become lean in order to become insulin sensitive (*i.e.*, obesity is not the underlying cause of the syndrome). Also, one does not have to be obese to be insulin resistant. So many non-obese men and women in the world are insulin resistant and don't realise it.

Substantial improvements in insulin sensitivity can be changed in a matter of days or weeks, which explains why dramatic improvements in glucose tolerance, blood pressures, and blood lipids can be observed so quickly after starting an exercise programme or eating healthier foods. If we can accept the fact that metabolically fit and healthy bodies can come in all shapes and sizes, then the public health message becomes quite simple: be more physically active and consume a healthier diet.

As for exercise, moderate-to-vigorous activity (heart rate in the range of ~60-75 per cent of maximum) for ~20-40 minutes per day on most days of the week is suitable for improving metabolic fitness (*9, 23*). Intensity and duration of exercise can be modified to suit individual needs. If time is not a constraint, duration can be emphasised while exercising at the lower end of the intensity range.

Just as effective, however, is high-intensity exercise of only 20-30 minutes duration. As for nutrition, the best foods to boost metabolic fitness are those you find primarily near the food guide pyramid: Whole grains, fruits and vegetables, and legumes (beans). These foods have plenty of fibre and have been shown to improve health regardless of weight and independent of weight loss.

Road to Fitness

It may seem intuitive that exercising more and eating better will naturally result in weight loss. This generally is true, but with a major caveat. Not everyone will lose weight, and it is virtually impossible to tell how much any one person will lose. Most exercise programmes and typical diets result in a weight loss of not more than 3 to 5 kg (32); the average "overweight" adult wants to lose 10 to 15 kg! This discrepancy between what people want and what exercise and healthy eating are able to deliver highlights the fundamental problem with using weight loss or reductions in body fat to judge the success of an exercise programme or nutrition plan.

Exercise and healthy eating should not be viewed merely as means to an end (weight loss), but rather as having their own intrinsic value. If someone quits an exercise programme out of failure to reach a particular weight loss (or reduced body fat) goal, then all the benefits of the exercise are lost as well. And far too many people who start exercise programmes don't stay with them. Yo-yo fitness is becoming as common as yo-yo dieting.

In developing countries today lakhs of men and women (and boys and girls) stigmatised as "too fat" are engaged in a perpetual war with their bodies. Isn't it about time we called a truce? Let's face biological reality. Some people are naturally meant to be thin, some naturally meant to be fat. Exercise and diet can modify our genetic destiny only so much.

The human body is not an infinitely malleable mass of calories that can be burned down to any shape and size desired. But that doesn't mean we can't all be as metabolically fit as our lifestyle will allow. In terms of health and longevity, the scientific evidence is abundantly clear: It is far more important to be fit than it is to be thin. Contrary to prevailing dogma, the road to a fitter and healthier body is not so narrow after all.

Difference between Living Well and Living

Quality of life is what we all want. Good health helps us achieve a high quality of life. Fitness makes us want to live it every day. If you agree with these three premises, keep reading.

The Purpose of Health and Fitness Tips: To inform you of new developments in the health and fitness fields is our aim. We'll do the research; we have the resources. You get the results. The name of the game is 'current' and 'relevant' for today. Forget all the excess baggage of the so-called fitness gurus.

Become Healthier and Fitter Faster: While we know you are interested in becoming healthier and fitter or maintaining the health and fitness you have, we also know you have limited time to devote to it. We therefore pledge to you a fast, simple method to hop aboard the fitness fast train. Get on track with the facts.

Health Professionals, Medical Experts and Health and Fitness Writers and Editors Make-up Our Staff: They all experience in the booming Health and Fitness field. Not that anyone is age 100 or even close, but we all plan to live that long. We want to make sure we have company. So we invite you along for the ride. We'll spur you on and help you over the rough spots to your own fitness destination.

Diet and Exercise are Keys to Healthy Living: But you know all this. So our aim is to give you the shortcuts, the little-known tricks and proven methods to help prevent boredom and hopelessness in your quest for good health. Our high tech world has advanced in the fitness field also. In fact, so fast that we want to get the information out to you yesterday. That's what the Health and Fitness Tips Site is all about...the latest up-to-the-minute-in-the-zone information for your health and fitness.

Tone Your Body, Tone Your Mind

People who love working out, but can't seem to stop stressing out, need to know that it is possible to get a sweat on and at the same time reduce their stress. Of course, this can come naturally over the course of heavy work-out when our body releases endorphins in the form of "runner's high," or through the euphoria we can attain when we reach difficult fitness goals.

But more focused approaches exist. As a whole health consultant, I recommend to readers any of these five great paths to stronger muscles and a more peaceful mind:

Peace of Mind

Stronger Muscles

1. Power Yoga is great for those seeking to combine a cardio work-out with the well-known, mind-calming benefits of regular yoga practice. The term "power yoga" originally was just a catchy synonym coined about ten years ago for a variation of Ashtanga yoga, but is now more broadly considered to be a series of physically challenging poses in no set order. Power yoga develops strength and flexibility while keeping you on the move. At the same time, it emphasises balancing body, mind and spirit like other yoga forms. Since classes can differ, I recommend talking to instructors before signing up with a particular class to make sure it provides enough of a relaxation focus for you.
2. Martial Arts are famous, of course, for cultivating mental and spiritual discipline while building physical strength

and agility. It is beyond the scope of this article to describe the many styles of martial arts practised in the world, but I suspect that fitness enthusiasts might find more gratification from practising "hard" (or "external") styles such as Karate, Tae Kwon Do, and Kickboxing, than the "softer" (or "internal") styles of T'ai Chi and Aikido, although the latter are typically more meditative.

Martial arts instruction can vary enormously on the extent to which they emphasise the self-defence, meditative, dance, exercise, spiritual, or energetic aspects of their style. Moreover, instruction can be very formal and traditional, or more relaxed and westernised. I strongly recommend sitting in on a class before signing up, and asking the instructor about their teaching philosophy to see how much it emphasises stress reduction.

3. NIA, stands for Neuromuscular Integrative Action. While it is not as well-known as Power Yoga, it has become a fashionable form of mind-body exercise. NIA is difficult to define, as it is a hybrid exercise that combines elements of martial arts, healing arts, and dance. Unlike power yoga, the NIA Technique can adapt itself more easily to all levels of physical ability. In a typical NIA class, participants are barefoot and are led through a series of movement exercises set to eclectic and energising music. Instructors encourage a mindful, healing attitude to the exercises, emphasising the joy of movement, emotional catharsis, free expression, and healing visualisation, in a sense taking the class on a journey towards greater self-awareness while getting a good workout at the same time.

4. The Roth Five Rhythms™ is a form of ecstatic dance developed by the artist, dancer and healer Gabrielle Roth. As a dancer, Roth discovered that people can experience emotional release, greater mind-body awareness, and healing when taken through a series of

five dance-movements: the graceful, loose and flexible flowing; the fiery, angular and passionate staccato; the wild and uncontrolled chaos; the soulful, stylish lyrical; and finally, the wise, inspiring and compassionate stillness.

Roth's stated philosophy is "Put your psyche in motion and it will heal itself". Five Rhythms™ classes take participants on a very personal and self-expressive journey through these rhythms, which can be a strenuous work-out for those in need of one.

5. You might find it odd for me to add Fencing to this list, but as Syd Fadner, Director of the Boston Fencing Club, points out, "Fencing is a sport that challenges mind, body and spirit. A combat sport that requires tactical thinking, emotional resiliency and physical conditioning, fencing encompasses a unique combination of fine motor skills and adrenal response. Students learning the sport of fencing develop focus, balance and endurance, while learning to respond effectively to the challenges of competition. It is sometimes described as chess at a hundred miles an hour."

A western cousin of Asian martial arts sword forms, fencing's adherents argue that one need not go around the world to find a form of vigorous exercise that cultivates the mind. Getting started in fencing is easy, and does not require owning sword (or a chandelier!).

Before you go out and sign up with any class, though, remember that we can cultivate calmness and peace of mind in whatever we do, whether its kickboxing, walking, or just washing the dishes. Whenever we choose a hard and strenuous physical activity, we should take a moment and try to see the softness and gentleness that lies inside of it. Not only might we find there the relaxation we seek, but this awareness may also take us to a higher level of performance and a deeper appreciation for balance in all aspects of our lives.

Better Health

Finances, Relationships and Mental Well-being!: The quality of your life is directly related to your standards. A standard is a personal rule or expectation about the level of excellence you require in something, and when you raise your standards you change your life.

In my work as a professional coach, I've found that most people haven't taken time to define their standards. Invariably, they've inherited rules from others, leading them to live their lives using someone else's game plan, If you'd like to improve the quality of your life, consider increasing your standards.

Your Model of Interaction: Your Model of Interaction dictates how you engage with people, and is related to who you believe you are. If you identify yourself an impatient person, you'll treat others with impatience. If you identify yourself as kind, you'll interact with others in a kind manner.

The law of reciprocity dictates that you will receive what you put out into the world. If you find yourself on the receiving end of uncooperative, negative behaviour, it might be time to take a look in the mirror. If you already treat the people in your life with warmth and kindness, then you're ahead of the game. Take a moment to define standards for how you'll interact with others.

Your Ability to Keep Your Word: Your personal integrity is related to your ability to do what you say you'll do. When you make a commitment, then you fail to follow through, you diminish your credibility and undermine your self confidence. When you follow through on your commitments, your credibility and self esteem increases. The level of faith you have in your own ability to follow through on commitments will directly impact the quality of your life. You'll be much more prepared to take risks when you have a high level of belief in yourself, and your willingness to risk is integral to your ability to tap into your potential. Before you commit to something, make sure it fits within the framework of your life. If it doesn't, don't commit. If you commit, follow through. Set yourself up to win, and believe in your ability to keep your word.

The White Space in Your Life: White space is an open playing field. Its uncommitted time. When you define standards to govern how you'll spend your time, the quality of your life increases exponentially. When you include a requirement to schedule uncommitted time, your stress level will decrease exponentially. This supports you in embracing your responsibilities, rather than resenting them. Spend a few moments defining a standard to create white space in your life.

Your Physical Health and Vitality: Do you like the way that you look and feel? Realise that whatever you might be dissatisfied with is the result of the behavioural standard you've set for yourself. If you want to change your appearance or energy level, it's imperative to define standards of behaviour that support your aspirations. Set some standards that guide how you'll care for yourself!

Your Financial Position: Your financial reality is directly related to your financial standards. Wealthy people have a different set of behavioural standards than people who struggle financially. What financial realities do you find acceptable? Do you think it's okay to have credit card debt? Do you require yourself to save? Have you established spending norms, or a process to use when making buying decisions? Take a few moments to define your financial standards.

Your Attitude: Your attitude is your disposition or frame of mind. It's how you see the world. In order to create the reality of your dreams, you must believe your dreams are possible. How are you going to approach your life? Will you allow yourself to honestly assess your reality? Will you believe you can impact your life? Will you require yourself to make the improvements required to develop the life of your dreams? Set those standards now.

Your Community: Nothing will sabotage your efforts to live a quality life more conclusively than surrounding yourself with people who don't support your standards. The most difficult course you'll navigate as you make life improvements will be terminating relationships with people who aren't equipped to grow with you, and reassuring those who are. Your relationships have the capacity to tear you down or lift you up. Surrounding yourself with people who share similar standards is an incredibly powerful way to create a lifestyle that pulls you toward your highest potential.

Surrounding yourself with people who don't support your standards will almost surely degenerate the quality of your life. Take a moment to consider the key people in your life. Do they conduct themselves in ways you respect? Do they support you and celebrate your successes? These are the people you should treasure and invest in. If they don't, you may want to reconsider sharing your life with them. What standard will you hold for the people in your life? Your standards act as the framework for your life. Increase your standards, improve your life!

6

Diet Plan

Are you confused with recent headlines? Actual headlines like:

Fat Is Back To Stay

Go Ahead and Have An Egg

Protein Is Back

Hold the Pasta Pass the Fat

Carbohydrates for High Energy Action

Pasta for the Soul and the Heart

If the answer is yes, welcome to the human race. You are not alone but I hope to help you make some sense of it all in this little dissertation.

Throughout recorded history, mankind has attempted to alter or control his diet to elicit optimum performance, body shape and health. Apparently, even the famous gladiators of ancient Rome ate preparations of fresh ground lions teeth and raw meat as a pre-performance meal in hopes of performing like a lion.

Volumes have been written extolling the virtues of a multitude of food and beverage choices, combinations, quantities, and timing, all designed to enhance exercise performance in some way.

What to Eat?

Modern research methods, science, technology and desire have combined to continue to develop some of the answers to this burning question.

We now exercise, outside of our vocation and procurement of life's basic necessities, for a variety of reasons. Scientific evidence suggests the reasons include: weight control, cardiovascular health (often by medical prescription), muscular development for looks and function, preparation for athletic competition and just plain fun.

We also know that carbohydrates provide quick energy, proteins build muscle, accumulated excess fat is unhealthy, water and electrolytes are necessary to prevent dehydration. Unfortunately there may be many finer points about these facts which most exercise enthusiasts and their well meaning advisors do not really understand. The human trend is to follow "the some is good, therefore more is better" or "some is bad, so none must be good" syndromes.

The Guidelines

During heavy exercise, the body produces more free-radicals—a natural and functional process. In excess, free radicals have been implicated as a cause of everything from cancer to heart disease. Protection from free radical damage is now strongly recommended by most health professionals.

Increased consumption of anti-oxidant nutrients (known as free radical scavengers) particularly vitamins C & E, Vitamin A (in the form of Beta Carotene) and other recently identified carotenoids like Alpha Carotene, lycopene from tomatoes and grape seed extracts provide protection.

Apparently as high as 40 per cent of marathon finishers, show some illness signs in the week following their race. The theory is that with the intensity and duration of the event, the immune system can become depleted through free radical attacks, unless we take extra precautions to help prevent the consequences. This would include consuming more anti-oxidants and protein in the form of foods and supplements.

Carbohydrate drinks and carbohydrate loading (the act of dramatically increasing carbohydrate intake a few days to hours prior to endurance performance) have received considerable attention over the last 30 years.

The theory, based on some convincing clinical research, is that in order to prolong intense endurance activity, one needs to increase glycogen storage in muscles to the maximum level so that available quick energy does not become a limiting factor.

Unless the activity extends well beyond an hour of high intensity exercise, muscle glycogen depletion will not be the limiting factor. In fact, excess stored glycogen may cause a temporary weight gain due to obliged water storage dictated by glycogen or simply fat storage due to elevated insulin in response to elevated carbohydrate intake.

It is also possible that high intake of carbohydrates can inhibit the body's ability to mobilise fat for energy and actually lead to hypoglycemia and lean tissue loss. Carbohydrate loading is not required for activities lasting under one hour.

Fat is the substrate (food source for energy metabolism) of choice by our active cells. In fact, if you are currently sitting quietly and reading this item, 75-85 per cent of your energy is coming from fat, unless you are downing a coke, beer, coffee or some other source of blood sugar elevating commodity. Even during moderate exercise, most of your energy comes from fat.

Required Knowledge

According to Dr. Norman Kaplan, from the University of Texas South-western Medical Centre and author of Clinical Hypertension, most overweight people are hyper insulinemic (too much insulin released into the bloodstream). Insulin is the storage hormone released by the pancreas when blood sugar rises.

The only way to control insulin levels is to control the rate and level of blood sugar elevation. The only way to do that, is to reduce the intake of refined or simple carbohydrate (including most so called whole grain products). Moderate to strenuous exercise does lower insulin for short periods of time.

High carbohydrate diets can promote hypoglycemia, even in the physically active, and the elevation of triglycerides (a heart disease risk factor). Remember that carbohydrate depletion in the muscles is usually not the limiting factor to continued quality exercise performance, unless the activity exceeds 75 minutes at 80+ per cent of aerobic capacity. Triglycerides are the most abundant fatty substance in the body, making up most of your stored fat.

A triglyceride is made of one half a sugar molecule (glycerol) with three fatty acids attached. When levels of triglycerides in the blood go up, they are considered a negative risk factor to clogged arteries. The solution? Reduce the intake of insulin stimulating carbohydrates and exercise regularly.

Fat in storage is reduced in two ways. First, it can be metabolised as an energy source through moderate intensity exercise (from sleeping to conversational intensity exercise). Second, there is a concept of Ketosis where incompletely metabolised fat molecules are released into the blood and removed through the kidneys. Ketosis occurs only when one is on a severely restricted carbohydrate diet. This is how the Atkins Diet and the Protein Power Diet work. Contrary to popular belief—dietary induced ketosis is not considered dangerous according to Dr. Calvin Ezrin of the UCLA division of Endocrinology and author of the Endocrine Control Diet (an Atkins style diet).

Fat mobilisation (removal from storage for use in energy metabolism) can be inhibited in two ways. First is through the elevation of blood insulin in response to carbohydrate consumption.

The second is though the elevation of blood lactic acid which occurs in response to intense (anaerobic) exercise. The solution? To reduce fat in storage, control your insulin with a reduction in simple or refined carbohydrate intake and participate in conversational intensity exercise for about 4 hours per week (Try not to do the 4 hours all on the same day.)

There is evidence, some recently published in the Journal Medicine & Science in Sports & Exercise by a group from New York State University in Buffalo and by another group in New Zealand, demonstrating that higher fat diets (up to 50 per cent fat) can improve endurance performance without negative effects on immune functions nor blood lipid parametres. Once again a suggestion that carbohydrate emphasis may be over done.

Muscle is the most metabolically active tissue. The more muscle you have the more fat you metabolise. (Seems unfair doesn't it? The more fit burn fat faster.)

Carbohydrates should make up 40 per cent of your calories. These are low Glycemic Index (a measure of how fast they raise blood sugar) carbohydrates like vegetables, except for corn and potatoes. Also emphasise fruit except for bananas and dried fruits.

Protein should make up 30 per cent of your calories. I emphasise high quality digestible protein sources including soy and selected whey protein drinks. Always eat protein at every meal and every snack—no exceptions.

Eat some of your protein foods first to further control the rate of the rise in blood sugar. Protein requirements range from 0.75 grams per ½ kg of desirable weight for the sedentary to 1.0 gram per ½ kg of desirable weight for the physically active.

Fats should also make up 30 per cent of your calories. Emphasise the good fats which includes nuts, seeds, avocados, olives, cold pressed oils, and supplements like lecithin capsules (never granules nor liquid due rancidity issues), GLA and EPA capsules.

It is these good fats in the proper insulin controlled environment that will produce optimum levels of all your important hormones. Never eat cheap hydrogenated oils, deep fried grease and margarine of any kind in an attempt to avoid the notorious trans fatty acids.

Consume saturated fats in moderation but don't be so paranoid as to exclude them. A responsible intake of essential fatty acids will balance out any potential negative effects of saturated fats. Cholesterol consumed has nothing to do with blood cholesterol levels. In fact elevated insulin from too many carbohydrates will stimulate the liver to make more cholesterol and cause more harm than eating eggs or other animal fat sources.

Responsible supplementation is no longer an option if optimal health is desired. In addition to lots of protein, vegetables, fruit, modest intake of whole grains, and essential fats, you need to prop up your nutritional arsenal with a well planned supplement programme. Oh yes, don't forget to exercise and drink lots of pure water.

Menu Planning

Following a long winter (for some all winters are long), many families are looking forward to the warmer "outdoor" season. You know–the season when we say "Let's spend an entire day outdoors performing demanding physical tasks" like hiking, climbing, bicycling, roller-blading, or gardening.

To get the most enjoyment from these high energy burning tasks, it is wise to make plans about the fuel to be consumed throughout the day to help provide a steady supply of this energy.

Proper food selection for an all-day hike or aggressive day in the garden can mean the difference between total enjoyment and "bonking" at 11:00 AM or 2:30 PM. "Bonking" is a term for really low blood sugar, very low energy and feeling like your world is in painful slow motion.

Unwise but common advice given to those wishing to maintain high energy expenditure levels would include the consumption of sugar loaded snack bars, energy bars, soda pop, popular sport drinks (which are really just non-carbonated pop with some table salt added), rice cakes, bananas, raisins and dried fruits. These choices are unwise because they all raise blood sugar very quickly (which does give you a temporary energy boost) resulting in an insulin surge from the pancreas.

A small, slow rise in insulin is both desirable and necessary because that is how the sugars go from the blood to the working cells to provide the basis for energy production. However, a "surge", which is how the pancreas responds to a sharp rise in blood sugar, causes blood sugar to drop quickly (often to levels below the pre-eating stage) creating the desire to sleep or not think too clearly or to be depressed. We call this "Hypoglycemia". Hunger is also prevalent with chronically elevated insulin.

Food choices for optimum energy and feelings of "well-being" involve the control of insulin. To avoid the peaks and valleys in energy and to maintain a happy level of vigour throughout a long day it is wise to:

(a) eat a varied diet with adequate protein and fat in addition to the carbohydrates,

(b) eat small meals and snacks to sustain the flow of energy, and

(c) maintain good levels of hydration by drinking liquids frequently.

Understand that at mild to moderate levels of exercise intensity you receive 50 to 75 per cent of your energy from stored fat. A mixed diet – and one prefers 40 per cent complex carbohydrate, 30 per cent protein and 30 per cent good fat– will prevent insulin surging and prevent hypoglycemia.

Eating protein and fat in every meal and every snack is the key to insulin control. So avoid the unwise list previously mentioned and create some menus from the following:

Breakfasts: Eggs, omelet's with cheese and or meat, large flake oatmeal, protein supplement drinks (not in juice), rye bread, sprouted wheat bread, fish, ham, back bacon.

Lunches: Egg salad, cottage cheese, yogurt (unflavoured), smoked salmon, pickled herring, peanut butter (no sugar), hard boiled eggs, beef or turkey jerky (home-made is best), cheese, apples, berries, coleslaw, sliced cold roast beef, chicken, turkey and rye bread or sprouted wheat bread.

Dinners: Choices of meat, poultry, fish (BBQ is great), salads, colourful vegetables – raw or stir fried, cottage cheese, tofu stir fries, yogurt (plain).

Snacks: Cheese, nuts, seeds, beef or turkey jerky, apples with cheese, yogurt, high protein sport bars, peanut butter bars.

Drinks: Avoid caffeine beverages, because they are dehydrating. Drink a cup of liquid (preferably not coffee, tea, pop, or booze), approximately every hour (more often if the activity is high intensity and the outdoor temperature is high).

Successful Marathoners and tri-athletes drink a cup every 15 minutes to avoid dehydration. Do not wait until you are thirsty, that is too late.

Try iced herbal tea, unsweetened, quality sport drinks that are primarily malto-dextrin sugars and contain 4 or more electrolytes (not just table salt), dilute fruit juices with meals and snacks are OK and of course water.

Some simple and wise planning of your food choices for the day will make your outdoor experiences memorable for all the right reasons.

Supplementation

Responsible supplementation is no longer an option if your objective is optimal health. Some health magezines publishes, on a regular basis, Recommended Nutrient Intake values to help guide us to appropriate levels for fat and protein intake along with many of the known or recognised vitamins and minerals. (Notice-there is no RNI for carbohydrates) Many health advisors try to tell their clients that they only need a "well balanced" diet to meet these recommendations. However if you do some careful arithmetic you will find the task very difficult.

Then if you read Dr. Shari Leiberman's book *"The Real Vitamin and Mineral Book"* in which she uses a term "Optimal Daily Intake" (ODI), you will find the task even more difficult.

The ODI is based on the latest research and reflects what our industrialised world has done to the air, water and food; in terms of quality and pollutants. This column will be in defence of the dogmatic opening statement "supplementation is no longer an option".

Nutritional supplementation is one of the fastest growing industries in the developing countries. Like all rapidly growing industries, the market place can become a consumer's night mare with a myriad of choices, a range of quality and some over zealous misleading marketing claims.

Although Health department attempts to provide some standards and controls, there are still many unregulated areas. These include many herbal products which are relatively unregulated and don't even require DIN (drug identification number) registration like all vitamin and mineral supplements.

The Health department also has difficulty in maintaining recognition of supplementation for therapeutic reasons. Then there are numerous products that do not require registration, are harmless but useless and some that have proven to be both harmful and useless. So the market place is still a "consumer beware" environment.

Why Supplement?

1. In the early 1900's, all produce (100 per cent) was organic. Rutgers University has published several papers comparing the nutrient density of organic produce and commercially grown produce. Organic always wins.
2. According to a US Department of Agriculture paper the average Calories intake in the early 1900's was 3800 Calories but today the average intake is only 1800 Calories. Less than half—and most is not organic. So we tend to eat less than half the nutrients each and every day.
3. Risk of "free radical" damage is much higher today as the industrial world contaminates our food, water and

air. We also produce free radicals during physical and psychological stress. Free radicals are bio-chemical units that, in excess, will destroy healthy cells unless we protect ourselves with adequate nutrition.

4. With average fat intake falling to 32 per cent of Calories (compared to 48 per cent in 1900), it becomes more difficult to get the Essential Fatty Acids (EFA's) from our diet. EFA's are responsible for encouraging fat metabolism and the creation of some "super hormones" that lead to the production of anti-inflammatory hormones. Processed food tends to alter or eliminate the EFA's.
5. Wide use of antibiotics has lead to the destruction of "friendly bacteria" in the intestine. Friendly bacteria, like acidophilus and bifidus play a big role in digestion and in maintaining the health of the colon.
6. A low Calorie intake is associated with a reduced fibre intake. The American Cancer Society recommends a daily fibre intake of 30 grams but average person eats only 12–15 grams per day. Such a low intake increases the risk of colon cancer and other toxic side effects.
7. Most people do not consume enough complete, high quality protein, particularly at breakfast and lunch. (There is a tendency to eat more protein than can be absorbed during the evening meal). Therefore I have become a big fan of Soy Protein Isolate supplementation at breakfast, lunch, during snacks and just before exercise. A modern solution to a modern problem.

What to Use?

In my nutritional coaching practice, I divide supplementation into the following categories:

(a) *Nutritional Supplements*—basic nutrients found in the Recommended Nutrient Intake tables.

(b) *Herbal Supplements*—which are really nature's medicine, designed to prevent and/or solve certain health problems. Few are designed for long term consumption.

(c) *Fibre Supplements*—fibre is indigestible but necessary for detoxification and regularity. It is not really a nutrient.

(d) *Protein Supplements*—self-explanatory.

(e) *Friendly Bacteria*—some now refer to these tiny organisms as "pro-biotics".

Considering the Why Supplement list and the above categories, the following is a responsible supplement Programme that would benefit the heath of all people. This is basic, minimal and designed primarily for prevention of ailments and maintenance of good health.

1. High Quality Multiple Vitamin/Mineral should include all 8 recognised B vitamins including biotin. Balanced in proportion to the RNI. This multi should also contain high levels of Calcium and Magnesium.
2. Anti-Oxidants—Vitamin in the form of mixed carotenoids like alpha, beta and gamma carotene; Vitamin C, at least 1,000 mg in a sustained release format; Vitamin E in the mixed tocopherol format supported with selenium and grape seed extract.
3. Fibre Supplement containing a mixture of soluble and insoluble fibres.
4. Protein Supplement–preferably a Soy Protein isolate—not only to obtain extra protein but to also take advantage of the phytonutrients known as isoflavones.
5. Friendly bacteria–acidophilus and bifidus.

Various Considerations

Responsible nutrition consultants may recommend other supplements for therapeutic reasons. The key word is "responsible". Their recommendations will include the use of products from reputable companies. The best products are from companies that conduct true, publishable clinical research. They would be proud of such research and be prepared to share it with you upon request.

Peanut Butter or Pasta?

Peanut butter or pasta? That is the question asked by many endurance performers as they read some of the new sports nutrition research literature. Following decades of athletes subscribing to the gospel of carbohydrate loading, a new paradigm is raising questions.

Is Fat the Fuel of the Future?

Research published by groups in Denmark, Buffalo, New York, Australia and South Africa are all placing a favourable twist to the concept of "fat loading" as a functional option to carbohydrate loading.

The Danish study reported that the running time to exhaustion, on an 80 per cent of Max VO2 task, was similar in both the high fat diet and the high carbohydrate diet groups following 4 weeks of training while on their respective diets. It also showed, through respiratory exchange ratio (RER) measurements, that the high fat group increased their energy expenditure from fat as training progressed—suggesting an adaptation in progress.

The Buffalo, NY studies showed similar results with no negative blood chemistry indicators indicated.

South African studies compared a high fat group to a high carbohydrate diet group on three types of exercise performance. As expected, during short periods of high intensity (anaerobic type) exercise there were no differences. However, when exercised to exhaustion, differences appeared. The high carbohydrate group lasted 50 per cent longer on high intensity bicycle exercise tests than the high fat group.

At moderate intensity exercise the high fat group cycled 87 per cent longer than the high carbohydrate group. The latter probably represents the recreational marathoner, the ultra marathoner or the Iron Man competitor whereas the former represents the competitive marathoner. (An intuitive observation not a scientific fact.)

As more studies on the subject appear, the investigations are focussing on the how and why does this happen, at what intensities is the information applicable and does the type of fat make a difference. There are also observations centred on the suggestion that a high fat diet triggers the production of aerobic related enzymes in muscle which allows for more aerobic energy to be available. (There is no anaerobic mechanism for fat metabolism.) There is also speculation that fat loading increases the amount of intra-muscular (between the muscle fibres) fat which is more available for metabolism than the subcutaneous fat and that serves to spare muscle glycogen for longer periods.

I have no conclusions to offer yet. Simply stay tuned with an open mind as this subject unfolds. And remember that muscle glycogen depletion is only a limiting factor in endurance events lasting over 1.5 hours at relatively high intensity. I know of ultra marathoners who consumed peanut butter from the jar during a race.

Happy running while you wonder.

Re-Shaping Diet

When the decision arrives that it is time to get fit the diet may or may not receive attention. This attention is manifest in several forms:

1. I am exercising more therefore I just need to eat more calories so I have the energy to continue. These are the people who believe it doesn't matter what you eat as long as you "burn" it off. This attitude shows a serious

disregard for the understanding of human nutrition requirements and there are many examples of failure from this attitude.

Or

2. I am exercising more so I must be sure to consume adequate nutrition to build, recover and avoid illness. This is the sensible attitude but often full of misconceptions about what is healthy and wise.

Or

3. I am exercising like an athlete so I need to start using those special Sports Nutrition products advertised in the magazines. This may be true but don't believe everything the ads say and understand that no single product is going to be the solution to all your problems.

Some or part of each of these scenarios is correct. Naturally I will explain which parts and add a few caveats and details.

So let's begin with understanding that Nutrition for exercise and sport begins in the grocery store and your kitchen. You require a plan and some understanding of what the body needs in the way of nutrients to optimise health and performance. Here is a list of concepts to use as guiding lights to understand your nutritional needs.

1. During rest and mild to moderate exercise (the kind of exercise in most fitness Programmes) 65-85 per cent of our energy metabolism is from fat. Fat is the "energy source" of choice.
2. Even during Marathon pace and duration, at least 50 per cent of the energy is from fat.
3. The only time high carbohydrate diets and carbohydrate loading may be implicated is during very long and intense exercise (in excess of 1½ hours). Then and only then is muscle glycogen depletion a limiting factor and correcting such depletion requires extra carbohydrates.

4. Chronically high carbohydrate diets lead to chronically elevated insulin levels (the fat storage hormone) and that leads to:

   (a) Weight gain

   (b) Elevated:

   (i) Cholesterol

   (ii) Tri-glycerides

   (iii) Blood pressure

   (c) Inflammatory conditions

   (i) Eczema

   (ii) Psoriases

   (iii) Migraines

   (iv) Asthma

   (v) Arthritis

5. We require a supply of good fats (Essential Fatty Acids or EFA's) to metabolise other fats and to avoid the inflammatory problems just listed. If fat intake falls below 30 per cent of calories there is no way one can get the EFA's required. Beware of low fat diets.

6. Not all "Sports Nutrition" products are needed, wise nor safe. Nutrition refers to nutrients required for performance like walking, talking, thinking and exercising, building and repair or recovery. Nutrition does not include un-natural—chemistry lab created concoctions that alter, over-stimulate or suppress natural processes and functions. Having said that, there are reliable and responsible Sports Nutrition products that are nutritious, natural, recommended and required. These include:

   (a) High quality protein supplements

   (i) Some designed to provide cell building material.

(ii) Some are meal replacements.

(iii) Some are designed for muscle glycogen recovery.

Each one is different and none can do all three functions.

(b) Energy bars or sports bars

(i) Some high carbohydrate versions do improve endurance performance.

(ii) Some are merely meal replacements.

(iii) Some of the higher protein versions are a convenient way to increase protein intake if required.

(c) Sports Drinks are designed to help replace fluid loss, electrolyte loss and provide extra carbohydrates when needed. There is a great range of quality here. The carbohydrate component of a quality drink will be "maltodextrin" (a glucose polymer) and the electrolyte list will contain 6–8 electrolytes like calcium, phosphorous, chloride, sodium, potassium, and magnesium, not just sodium and potassium.

7. There is no evidence that muscle glycogen (the muscle storage form of glucose) depletion is ever the limiting factor in performance in short (less than 1½ hours) term, sub-maximal intensity exercise. There is also no evidence that a muscle "full" of glycogen will out perform a muscle that is "half-full"–except in long, high intensity endurance events.

8. Exercise does increase "free radical" damage, which challenges our immune systems. (One survey showed that 35 – 40 per cent of Marathon finishers get sick within one week of the race completion). Our best-known free radical scavengers are the anti-oxidants like vitamins A, C, E plus beta-carotene, selenium and the "proanthocyanidins" found in grape seed extract. All this is a strong case for eating lots of colourful fruits and vegetables.

9. Responsible supplementation with vitamins, minerals, essential fatty acids, fibre and protein is not an option if you wish to experience optimal health, fitness and performance.

All of this means that the optimal diet for the healthy and fit will contain lots of colourful fruits and vegetables, lots of high quality proteins, responsible supplements and selective use of Sports bars and drinks.

My personal choice for food selection is an eating plan of 40 per cent carbohydrates (primarily from fruits and vegetables—less from grains), 30 per cent high quality protein (some from supplements) and 30 per cent fat (10 per cent essential fats—some from supplements, 10 per cent mono-unsaturated fat like olive oil and sesame oil and 10 per cent saturated fat). I also recommend a quality multi-vitamin/ mineral supplement, extra anti-oxidant supplements and some fibre supplementation.

Runner's Diet

When it comes to nutritional advice for sport and exercise there is always some new "magic bullet" product or plan designed to help you become the next super athlete.

This is not a new phenomena. Man has altered diets to enhance performance since ancient times. Many years ago, my Classics professor related the fact that the Gladiators were reported to have eaten ground lion's teeth and raw meat prior to a performance in an attempt to take on the ferocious characteristics of the lion and therefore improve their chances of success. An examination of a few nutritional practices and procedures associated with intended performance improvements seems warranted.

Health

The first consideration of every runner should be to eat as healthy as possible to ensure a strong immune system and thus prevent illness. One of the major contributors to ill health is "free-radical" damage to cells. Such damage can be the underlying cause of many forms of cancer, heart disease and other cellular damage. It is well established that among marathon finishers, 40 per cent experience some form of illness within one week of completing their race—a sign of a depressed immune system.

Free radical production is a natural occurrence during intense exercise. To prevent free radical damage one needs to eat more free radical scavengers known as "anti-oxidants"—beta carotene, other carotenoids, Vitamins C & E, selenium, lycopene, etc. obtained from fresh fruit, vegetables and supplements.

Optimum health is also dependent upon eating adequate high quality protein to produce those immune cells and obtaining enough "Essential Fatty Acids" (EFAs) to produce the super hormones which control all other hormones.

Higher protein requirements for runners are now being recognised by many nutrition coaches. Long distance runners may need more protein than body builders because they tend to "challenge" their bodies at high intensities longer.

Recent studies reported that women who obtained 24 per cent or more of their calories from protein, experienced significantly fewer heart and cardiovascular problems. Also, in a recent issue of the journal "Cancer" it was reported that women on higher protein diets experienced better breast cancer survival rates.

In the same study, contrary to many previous reports, fat intake including saturated fat had no bearing on the results. A study from the University of Buffalo has shown suppressed immune systems during very low fat diets. The American Hear Association has declared that fat intakes below

30 per cent of calories "are unfounded and potentially dangerous". Then there are innumerable studies showing the positive role of essential fatty acids (from nuts, seeds, cold pressed oils and supplements) in the prevention of heart disease, cancer and inflammatory conditions. Very low fat diets do not contain enough EFA's.

Preparation

Carbohydrate (CHO) loading and pre-event hydration have been the trend over the last 15 years in the sports nutrition literature.

Carbohydrate loading has been over done. This can account for the difficulty some have in losing weight, controlling their cholesterol, triglycerides, blood pressure or PMS to name a few problems. The role of CHO loading is to delay muscle glycogen depletion. Such depletion can be the limiting factor in successful completion of intense, long duration tasks.

However such depletion does not occur unless one performs at a very high percentage of capacity (75 per cent+ for over 90 minutes). This intensity is rare even for competitive marathoners. Yes, one can deplete glycogen during an intense marathon or triathlon but not during a sub one hour, sub-maximal work out. Most training sessions occur at an intensity of 50 to 65 per cent of capacity. During such intensities, 35 to 60 per cent of energy expenditure is still coming from fat.

Recent published studies from Denmark, Japan, New Zealand, England and the University of Buffalo have demonstrated success with a concept of "Fat Loading". Apparently there is adaptation to fat burning and it is as effective as CHO loading with the added advantage of not over stimulating insulin production which can set up immune challenges and inflammatory conditions.

I personally have completed two Marathons without CHO loading and following a 40-30-30 diet plan throughout training. There may still be rationale for using a high quality sport drink during and after long intense runs. This drink should be made from glucose polymers like maltodextrin and not table sugar sucrose plus a good level of at least 6 electrolytes, not just sodium and potassium. Sub one hour, sub maximal work-outs do not indicate the use of more than water, unless the environment is very hot.

Recovery

Once intense exercise is completed, recovery of spent glycogen and replacement of metabolised "Branched Chain Amino Acids" (leucine, isoleucine and valine) becomes the focus. Research from the University of Texas published in the early 90's, verified by others since, reported that drinking a carbohydrate (glucose polymer) mixed with a protein containing a high BCAA profile (whey protein isolate), in a ratio 3:1 in favour of CHO, provides optimum glycogen recovery and enhances muscle recovery. It reduces muscle soreness and reduces any feeling of "heavy legs" following exercise.

Depending on how long and intense the work-out—some re-hydration with the high quality sport drink may be indicated following exercise.

To feel your best, stay healthy, perform best and recover fast follow some of these guidelines.

1. Eat high "nutrient dense" fruits and vegetables to obtain antioxidants.
2. Eat high quality protein, approximately 1 gram/½ kg of desirable weight/day to help build healthy immune cells. Eat 20-30 grams of protein in the hour before training or competing. Never eat more than 35 grams of protein in a single meal.

3. Eat high quality nuts, seeds, cold pressed oils as sources of EFAs.
4. Supplement with Soy Protein isolate drinks, EFAs (lecithin, EPA, GLA, flax seed oil) and antioxidants.
5. Use a high quality sport drink during and after long, intense, hot environment runs.
6. Recovery Drinks (3:1 in favour of CHO) have shown excellent results.

Right Snack—Snack Right

Snaking in the morning, snaking in the evening, snaking any old time–might become a new consumer theme song. Recent surveys say that snaking is on the increase and this has brought forward a deluge of expert advice (including this column) on how to snack in a healthy way. Unfortunately much of this well-meaning advice is both incorrect and a prescription for nutritional disaster.

A "SNACK" by definition is "a small meal eaten between regular meals".

Today an entire industry has evolved around a concept of providing convenient, quick, no-preparation snacks. In earlier years snacks were prepared in a home kitchen and usually had some nutritionally sound redeeming qualities. Today most snacks are purchased and presented in a bag, box, bottle or plastic wrapper and they tend to have a lengthy, non-refrigerator shelf life with questionable nutritional value.

Healthy snacks are (not just can be) an integral part of a healthy way of eating. Experience and science show that to maintain good levels of energy—without sharp peaks and valleys–we should eat every three hours. We should also start the day with a responsible breakfast that helps to set blood sugar levels and hormone patterns for the day.

This absence of a good breakfast (that should include a reasonable serving of protein–more than a tablespoon of peanut butter or a single glass of milk) creates a spike in the blood sugar that raises insulin sharply and that causes blood sugar to drop quickly (we call it hypoglycemia) and leaves us hungry and can be the physiological explanation for the morning coffee break. These coffee breaks are the worst-case scenarios for poor choice snacks.

Upon recently reviewing several dozen articles and web pages on snacks I find that conventional wisdom is directing consumers to choose snacks that, although they contain vitamins and minerals, create insulin disasters. Chronically elevated insulin levels are responsible for chronic or frequent hunger, fat storage, inhibition of fat metabolism and a host of other health problems. I am referring to those conventional choices like dried fruit, muffins, bananas, boxed cereal, pretzels, bagels, dried fruit bars, many energy bars, popcorn, and rice cakes.

Wise, higher protein, higher fibre and essential fatty acid sources would include:

Small bag of almonds, cashews or pecans.

Half an apple (or other fruit choice) with one gram of cheddar cheese.

Half cup of plain 1 or 2 per cent yogurt.

Cottage cheese and fruit.

One gram of smoked salmon, shrimp, crab, or tuna on a high fibre cracker.

Beef jerky (preferably home made).

Hard-boiled egg and half an apple.

One cup of 1 per cent or 2 per cent milk and 6 almonds.

Any colourful, raw non-root vegetable with any of the above protein choices.

High protein "energy" bar.

Small soy protein drink mixed in milk or water never juice.

Plan your snacks and don't wait until you are hungry. Happy snaking.

Celebration Eating

Celebrations, special events, festivals are all times when we "indulge" in our favourite comfort foods. It has been suggested that the highest rate of absenteeism from school occurs one or two days following a special holiday. The reason suggested is that we tend to over eat or eat too many of the wrong things during such events and it overloads our immune system, which in turn, causes some form of illness. I dislike starting on the negative but it does serve to draw your attention to the concern.

Foods to Avoid

High sugar content foods are well known to suppress the immune system which makes you vulnerable to colds, flu and other infections. There is also the "empty calorie" issue in high sugar foods. They provide lots of calories but few nutrients. And of course, at the risk of sounding like a broken record, there is the issue of an over stimulated pancreas from the absorption of high sugar foods. This over-stimulated pancreas means you have too much insulin in the blood. This leads to excess fat storage, hypoglycemic reactions, inflammatory conditions (asthma, arthritis, psoriasis, eczema, migraines), yeast infections and hormonal imbalances and even depression. If you are interested in or concerned about your health it would be wise to control your insulin.

Chemical cocktails are the other foods to pay attention to. So talking about those with very long lists of ingredients containing many un-pronounceable words. Not only do these items challenge your immune system but for some people they contribute to behaviour changes (like the ADD child or adult) and many are known to be carcinogenic. In this category including the Trans Fatty acids—those fats that have been over heated.

Tans Fatty Acids have been implicated in many health problems including heart disease and cancer. Never eat deep fried grease, cheap oils or margarine of any kind.

Therefore, to avoid regretting your trip to the Stampede, minimise or avoid cotton candy, soda pop, doughnuts, slurpies, cheap ice cream, french fries and even the famous corn dog. Although it may be the least harmful of the list. Naturally you want to minimise alcohol because it can cause a real quick rise in insulin.

Chosen Foods

In order to control the insulin you want to eat protein in every meal and every snack and to eat some of the protein food first. Good choices would include beef on a bun but only eat half the bun. Choose to eat at some of the "complete meal" vendors and choose baked potatoes over French fries. Hamburgers (again half the bun), roast pork products, unsweetened milk products (look out for frozen and flavoured yogurts they are loaded with sugar).

Fruit smoothies can be OK, if they don't load them with sugar. Beef jerky is better than most hot dogs and local sausage will be better than commercial smokies. When you attend your Stampede breakfasts, be sure to get lots of meat or eggs and to eat some of the protein food first.

Control your urge to drown the pancakes in syrup (a little can allow the flavour of the pancake to come through). Actually the Stampede lunches and dinners are often a better choice. If you are serving your own Stampede breakfast consider serving whole wheat or oatmeal pancakes to your guests and provide some peanut butter and home preserve jam as an alternative to syrup.

You need to understand that sugars and starches, which raise insulin very fast, also help to increase your hunger and can make you lethargic or put you to sleep. On the other hand, protein foods control insulin and help to keep you alert and awake with lots of energy (not mention protecting your immune system).

Although it is a festival and a celebration, it need not become a nutritional and health disaster, to be enjoyed. Eat to stay healthy and alert and not to become ill and fall asleep.

7

Significance of Diet

Most peoples view a healthy lifestyle as something difficult to attain and something that's not much fun. Traditional diets have taught us that to lose weight, we must count calories, keep track of everything we eat, and deprive ourselves by limiting the amount and kinds of foods we eat. Diets tell us exactly what and how much food to eat, regardless of our preferences and individual relationships with hunger and satiety. Dieting can help us lose weight (fat, muscle, and water) in the short-term but is so unnatural and so unrealistic that it can never become a lifestyle that we can live with, let alone enjoy!

While very few diets teach healthy low-fat shopping, cooking, and dining-out strategies, many offer unrealistic recommendations and encourage health-threatening restrictions. Even more important, diets don't teach us the safest, most effective ways to exercise; they don't teach us how to deal with our cravings and our desires, or how to attend to our feelings of hunger and fullness. Eventually, we become tired of the complexity, the hunger, the lack of flavour, the lack of flexibility, the lack of energy, and the feeling of deprivation. We quit our diets and gain back the weight we've lost; sometimes we gain even more!

Each time we go on another diet of deprivation, the weight becomes more difficult to lose, and we become even more frustrated and discouraged. Then we eat more and exercise less, causing ourselves more frustration, discouragement, depression. Soon we are in a vicious cycle. We begin to ask ourselves, "Why bother?" We begin to blame ourselves for having no will power when what we really need is clear, scientifically-based information that will help us develop a healthier lifestyle we can live with for the rest of our lives.

Deliberate restriction of food intake in order to lose weight or to prevent weight gain, known as dieting, is the path that lakhss of people all over the world are taking in order to reach a desired body weight or appearance. Preoccupation with body shape, size, and weight creates an unhealthy lifestyle of emotional and physical deprivation. Diets take control away from us.

Many of us who diet get caught in a "yo-yo" cycle that begins with low self-acceptance and results in structured eating and living because we lack trust in our body and are unwilling to listen and adhere to our body's signals of hunger and fullness. On diets, we distrust and ignore internal signs of appetite, hunger, and our need to be physically and psychologically satisfied. Instead, we depend on diet plans, measured portions, and a prescribed frequency for eating.

As a result, many of us have lost the ability to eat in response to our physical needs; we experience feelings of deprivation, then binge, and finally terminate our "health" programme. This in turn leads to guilt, defeat, weight gain, low self-esteem, and then we're back to the beginning of the yo-yo diet cycle. Rather than making us feel better about ourselves, diets set us up for failure and erode our self-esteem.

The attitudes and practices acquired through years of dieting are likely to result in a body weight and size obsession, low self-esteem, poor nutrition and excessive or inadequate exercise. Weight loss from following a rigid diet is usually temporary. Most diets are too drastic to maintain; they are unrealistic and unpleasant; they are physically and emotionally stressful. And most of us just resume our old eating and activity patterns.

Diets control us; we are not in control. People who try to live by diet lists and rules learn little or nothing about proper nutrition and how to enjoy their meals, physical activity, and a healthy lifestyle. No one can realistically live in the diet mode for the rest of their life, depriving themselves of the true pleasures of healthy eating and activity.

We Don't Fail Diets; They Fail Us!

Decades of research have shown that diets, both self-initiated and professionally led, are ineffective at producing long-term health and weight loss (or weight control). When your diet fails to keep the weight off, you may say to yourself, "If only I didn't love food so much... If I could just exercise more often... If I just had more will power."

The problem is not personal weakness or lack of will power. Only 5 per cent of people who go on diets are successful. Please understand that we are not failing diets; diets are failing us.

The reason 95 per cent of all traditional diets fail is simple. When you go on a low-calorie diet, your body thinks you are starving; it actually becomes more efficient at storing fat by slowing down your metabolism. When you stop this unrealistic eating plan, your metabolism is still slow and inefficient that you gain the weight back even faster, even though you may still be eating less than you were before you went on the diet.

In addition, low-calorie diets cause you to lose both muscle and fat in equal amounts. However, when you eventually gain back the weight, it is all fat and not muscle, causing your metabolism to slow down even more. Now you have extra weight, a less healthy body composition, and a less attractive physique.

Diets require you to sacrifice by being hungry; they don't allow you to enjoy the foods you love. This does not teach you habits which you can maintain after the diet is over. Most diet programmes force you to lower your caloric intake to dangerously low levels.

The common theory is that if you eat fewer calories than you burn, you will lose weight. But when you eat fewer calories than your body needs to maintain its life-sustaining activities, you're actually losing muscle in addition to fat. Your body breaks down its own muscles to provide the needed energy for survival.

Traditional diets which use calorie restriction to produce weight loss are no longer appropriate. Most weight-loss programmes measure success solely in terms of the number of kgs lost per weight loss attempt.

Diets don't take into account the quality of the process used to achieve that weight loss or the very small likelihood of sustained weight loss. For long-term good health, you need to move away from low-calorie diets and focus on enjoyable physical activity and good nutrition. Exercising regularly and eating lean-supporting calories, protein and carbohydrates, and reducing fat-supporting calories will not only help you look and feel better, it will also significantly reduce your risk of disease.

If we focused more on prevention and on improving our day-to-day behaviours, we could cut health care costs in half. Contrary to popular belief, leading a healthy lifestyle doesn't have to be difficult; it doesn't have to painful or time-consuming. Making gradual, simple changes in your diet and physical activity will make great improvements in your health and well-being, and they can drastically reduce your risk of disease.

If your weight management programme is to be a success, everything you eat and every exercise you do must be a pleasurable experience. If you are not enjoying yourself, it is unlikely that you will continue your programme. It's that simple. These small, gradual changes are not painful or overwhelming but rather the core of an exciting lifestyle that you will look forward to.

Take the frustration, guilt, and deprivation out of weight management, and allow yourself to adopt gradual, realistic changes into your life that will make healthy eating and physical activity a permanent pleasure. You will soon discover what your body is capable of and begin to look, act, and feel your very best. Good luck and enjoy all the wonderful benefits of a healthy, active lifestyle.

Strength Training Principles and Guidelines

Almost any form of exercise will stimulate some degree of strength and muscle development. Unfortunately, misconceptions, myths, and misunderstandings plague the fitness industry, especially in regard to strength training. There is a huge attrition rate among those starting a strength-training Programme primarily because most people are not taught the principles essential for a safe and effective programme.

The following exercise guidelines are extremely important for your safety and the effectiveness of your strength-training programme.

Warming Up, Cooling Down and Stretching

Warming-up promotes safety, prevents injury, and increases performance. You should warm up two ways with the purpose of creating blood flow throughout the body and thus preparing your muscles for the work-out. First, before beginning your weightlifting session, do some form of cardiovascular exercise at a light, comfortable intensity for about five to ten minutes. Walking or riding a bicycle works well. When you've completed your warm-up, be sure to stretch the primary muscles you've been using. For example, if you warmed-up on the bicycle, stretch your quadriceps, hamstrings, calves, and hips.

Then, for the first exercise of each muscle group, do a warm-up set with very light weight for 12-20 repetitions. For example, if your first chest exercise is the bench press, do a warm-up set of very light weight and then continue with your selected chest routine. When you have completed your chest work-out and are ready to train the next muscle group, once again do a warm-up set; then continue training that muscle group, and so on.

Stretching provides better physical performance, prevents debilitating injuries, and makes you look and feel better by improving your posture. This is because when muscles are stretched, their elasticity improves, increasing your range of motion and improving the quality of your movements. Never stretch a cold muscle—always make sure your muscles are warm before stretching. When a muscle is properly warmed-up it is better able to become elastic and relaxes more easily; warming up also circulates blood to nearby tissues and helps remove unwanted waste products from your system.

In addition to stretching the muscles involved in the cardiovascular exercise, you should spend time stretching each specific muscle you have trained in your weightlifting programme. This won't take much more time and the benefits are many. You have to rest between your strength training sets anyway, so you might as well use this time more productively for stretching. Think about it: what better time to stretch than right after you have targeted blood to a specific muscle? After you have properly warmed up each muscle group, stretch between sets.

Each set requires a resting period—usually between 30 seconds and three minutes (depending on what you are trying to achieve). Use your resting time wisely and stretch the specific muscle being trained. Stretch only after the muscle has been properly warmed-up and about once every two to three sets per muscle group.

By the time you have finished training each muscle of the body, you will have incorporated stretching into your programme, and at the best possible time to stretch—right after exercise, when the muscle is warm. This stretching between exercises is a valuable technique and will make a tremendous difference in your health.

The cool-down after strength training is also crucial. Whenever a vigorous exercise session is stopped abruptly, blood tends to accumulate in the lower body. With reduced blood return, cardiac output decreases and light-headedness may occur. Because muscle movement helps squeeze blood back to the heart, it is important to continue some muscle activity after the last exercise is completed. Easy cycling, walking, or any other cardiovascular exercise at low intensity is an appropriate cool-down activity, as is any other form of cardiovascular exercise. Cool down for about 5-10 minutes at light intensity, similar to your warm-up.

We will discuss the importance of forcing blood to your muscles, common mistakes that hinder the process, and proper lifting speed. Until then, remember to always include a warm-up, stretching, and a cool-down for maximum effectiveness and to prevent injury. Good luck, and enjoy all the wonderful benefits of strength training.

Almost any form of exercise will stimulate some degree of strength and muscle development. Unfortunately, misconceptions, myths, and misunderstandings plague the fitness industry, especially in regard to strength training. There is a huge attrition rate among those starting a strength training programme primarily because most people are not taught the principles essential for a safe and effective programme.

This article discusses the very important principles and guidelines of a safe and effective strength training programme. This article discusses the importance of forcing blood to your muscles and proper lifting speed. The previous article, explained the proper methods of warming-up, stretching, and cooling-down for a safe and effective strength training programme. The following exercise guidelines are extremely important for your safety and the effectiveness of your strength training programme.

Importance of Blood Supply to Your Muscles

It is important to understand the value and purpose of targeting or forcing blood to the muscles you are training. Many of the principles we teach have the sole purpose of forcing blood into your muscles. When you use proper lifting technique, you will notice blood racing to the specific muscle you are training. And this is exactly what you want to happen.

When blood is forced into your muscles during your weightlifting programme it potentiates the "microtrauma" or tiny little tears in your muscles that we mentioned earlier. When this happens, your muscle tissues repair and rebuild themselves bigger and stronger than they were—if you allow ample resting time. This is why you never train the same muscle group two days in a row; if you do, you cut off the rebuilding process.

You will know that you are using proper form when you feel a warmth, some fatigue, and a "burning" feeling at the end of each set for each muscle group. If you do not get this feeling, you probably need to review the proper form for your exercise. This may be an indication that you are making other common mistakes in your routine that do not allow blood to be fully targeted to the your muscles.

One of the most common mistakes people make is not training their muscle groups in an organised, systematic fashion. Always do every set and every exercise for specific muscle groups together.

For example, if your chest routine consists of three sets of bench press, do all three sets, separated by resting periods, and then go on to the next muscle group. Or, if your chest routine consists of two or three different chest exercises, do all of those chest exercises together. Do the Bench Press, then incline Bench Press, then Flys, for example—until your chest routine is complete. Then you can move on to the next muscle group.

Many people make the mistake of doing a set of Bench Press for their chest, then a set of Biceps Curls, then another set of Bench Press, and then on to another muscle group, and so on. This does not fully target blood into any one muscle group. You are just teasing your chest muscles and then moving on to tease another muscle group without ever targeting enough blood into any muscle group to cause much stimulation for improvement.

Another common mistake is eating right before your training Programme or eating too soon after your programme. This can cause your heart and digestive system to work too hard and compromise the oxygen and nutrient delivery to the working muscles. Eating just before or too soon after your work-out will not allow you to get enough blood into the muscles you are training.

Think about this: Digestion takes a lot of blood to work effectively. The more blood your body sends to digest your food the less blood is available to go to your muscles, to rebuild and increase strength. You should wait at least 60 minutes after eating before you start your exercise programme.

Similarly, do not eat too soon after ending your work-out because you want the blood that you just targeted into each specific muscle to remain there as long as possible. If you eat food too soon after your work-out, the blood will be forced out of your muscles and into your digestive system. So wait at least 60 minutes after your programme before you eat a meal.

Of course you should not go to your work-outs hungry; you definitely want nutrients in your system for performance enhancement and energy, but try to eat an hour or more before work-outs, and make sure your meal includes foods that are rich in complex carbohydrates and protein and low in fat, sugar, and cholesterol.

Lifting Speed

One of the most important elements in weightlifting—one that has a big effect on how much blood is targeted to your muscles is lifting speed. Speed plays a major role in the incidence of injury as well as strength and muscle development. Fast lifting creates momentum and doesn't promote blood flow to the muscle. Slow movement creates less momentum and less internal muscle friction. Not only does slow lifting require a more even application of muscle power throughout the movement range, it actually promotes rapid blood flow into the specific muscle you are training.

In every strength training exercise for every muscle there are two different parts to each repetition of the exercise set performed. One, the concentric contraction called the "positive" phase of the repetition is the part where the muscle is actually doing the work, such as the lifting motion of the bicep curl from the beginning where your arms are hanging straight down to the point where the weight is lifted up. The second part is the eccentric contraction—called the "negative" phase of the repetition—is the part with resistance, because you are returning the weight from the end of the positive phase back to the beginning. In the bicep curl, this is where you let the weight come back slowly to the beginning position, with your arms extended straight down again.

It is more important to let the weight come back slowly on the "negative" phase than on the "positive" phase. Coming back slowly with resistance on every exercise is very, very important because this is the phase that promotes blood flow to your muscles and thus causes microtrauma, building your muscles even stronger during your day of rest.

We recommend one to two seconds for each lifting movement (the positive phase), and three to four seconds for each lowering movement (the negative phase). Whatever your actual lifting speed, remember to always come back slower with resistance (the negative phase) for each and every weightlifting exercise. If you find that the weight is so heavy that you cannot come back slowly in full control of the movement, you should lighten the weight until you can.

Many people pay far too much attention to the quantity or weight of the lift and not the quality of the movement performed. Your muscles cannot know how much weight is on the bar or machine, but they will respond very well when you are using good, controlled form and come back slowly with resistance.

This article discusses the very important principles and guidelines of a safe and effective strength training programme. This article discusses the importance of proper lifting technique, exercising through the full range of motion, proper exercise sequence, and the correct number of sets to do for what you're trying to achieve.

Form and Technique

The most common and critical training mistakes may be those of exercise technique. The tendency to use too much weight typically results in poor form, which decreases your ability to get results, and increases the risk of injury. Examples of poor form or technique are: bouncing the bar off the chest in the Bench Press; using hip and back extension to initiate Bicep Curls; arching the back or bending backward under Shoulder Presses; using any sort of momentum in any exercise; and training at fast speeds. These mistakes will not send the blood you need into your muscles and will work counter to your goals. Be aware of these mistakes and eliminate them from your programme.

Exercise through Full Range of Motion

Perform each exercise through a full range of motion, with emphasis on the end of the positive phase. Full range exercise movements are advantageous for strengthening the prime-mover, or agonist muscles—the muscles directly trained in the exercise, such as the Biceps in the Biceps Curl. Lifting in the full range of motion is also advantageous for stretching the antagonist muscles, the muscles that act in opposition to the agonist. In the Biceps Curl, the triceps is the antagonist. Training in the full range of motion enhances both muscle strength and joint flexibility.

Exercise Selection

It is very important to select at least one exercise for each major muscle group to promote well-balanced muscle development. Training only a few muscle groups or training one muscle group are more increases the risk of injury.

Exercise Sequence

Another important element of strength training is exercise sequence. When performing a variety of weightlifting exercises, it is advisable to proceed from the larger muscle groups to the smaller muscle groups. This allows optimal performance of the most demanding exercises when fatigue levels are the lowest and you feel fresh. Another reason, one that is often overlooked, is illustrated by the common example of training both back and biceps. Ordinarily, you would want to train your back first, since it is the larger muscle group of the two; let's say you are doing the Rear Lat. Pull-down. In that exercise, you are indirectly working your biceps, too, since both muscle groups are at work in the pulling motion.

This means that your biceps will actually be warmed up and ready to train when you get to them. This is the same for exercises requiring pushing motions such as the chest, shoulders, and biceps. By the time you are done with your chest exercises, both your shoulders and your biceps are warm and ready to train. Of course, you might not always do your "pulling" (back and biceps) and your "pushing" (chest, shoulders, biceps) motions on the same day—because as you reach a plateau you will want to change your exercises, the order that you do them, and the muscles that you train together, to provide a new stimulus and interest for yourself. This will be discussed soon.

Sets

Another important element is exercise sets. An exercise set is the number of successive repetitions performed without resting. The number of sets per exercise is largely a matter of goals, interests and personal preference. We recommend that people treat their first set as a warm-up—12-20 reps with relatively light weight (done slowly).

Then you can do either one, two, or three more sets—even up to six (strength and power programme)—depending on whether you are at a beginning, intermediate, or advanced level and what you are trying to accomplish.

If you are working on your second exercise for a particular muscle group, we recommend that you do either two or three sets for that exercise since that muscle is already warmed-up from the first exercise. Regardless of the number of sets performed, each set—and each repetition—should be done in proper exercise form and under control.

Now, the inverse relationship between resistance and repetitions and the importance of progressive resistance would be discussed. Here the amount of weight you should use and the number of repetitions you should do for the results you desire are explained.

It is explained how to gradually increase the weight you use to stimulate further gains. Until then, remember to use proper lifting technique, exercise through the full range of motion, exercise in the proper sequence, and use the correct number of sets for what you're trying to achieve. Good luck, and enjoy all the wonderful benefits of strength training.

This article discusses the amount of weight you should use and the number of repetitions you should do for the results you desire. And here it also explain how to gradually increase the weight you use to stimulate further gains.

Relationship between Resistance and Repetitions

It's important to understand the inverse relationship between exercise resistance and exercise repetitions. When exercising to the point of muscle fatigue, most people can complete about six repetitions with 85 per cent of maximum resistance. "Maximum resistance" is the most weight you can lift one time, in good form.

Most people can complete eight repetitions with 80 per cent of maximum resistance, 10 repetitions with 75 per cent of maximum resistance, and 12 repetitions with 70 per cent of maximum resistance.

For most people (those seeking muscle strength and tone), 8-12 repetitions with 70-80 per cent of maximum resistance is a sound training recommendation for strength and muscle development. Most people do not bother with finding their one repetition maximum for each lift to obtain the appropriate weight for each set of 8-12 repetitions. This would get pretty tedious especially when you are learning a new exercise.

Really, the best and easiest way to figure out how much weight you should use on each lift is to begin by taking your best conservative guess. After you have warmed up by using a light weight for 12 or 20 reps, choose a weight for your next set that will challenge you for your goal number of repetitions. If you are not sure what that weight should be, choose a weight that is likely to be too light, rather than making the mistake of going too heavy and not reaching your desired number of repetitions.

For example, say you are trying to decide the proper weight for a set of 12 repetitions on the Shoulder Press. Choose a light, conservative weight slightly heavier than your warm-up and do the set 12 times (repetitions or reps). When you come to your twelfth repetition, if you feel as though you can perform another repetition or two, while still using good form, you might as well do that (to further promote blood flow to the shoulder muscle).

Since you know that the weight you chose was a little too light (your 12th repetition was not a challenge), next time choose a slightly heavier weight that will challenge you for all twelve repetitions, or whatever your goal number of repetitions happens to be.

Important Note: Your strength may gradually decline as you progress through your routine. For example, on your first set (after warm-up) of the Bench Press you did 12 reps with 70 kg.—this would force a good amount of blood and fatigue your chest muscles. If for your second set you're trying to figure out the appropriate weight for 10 reps, you may or may not want to slightly increase the weight. That is, 70 kg. might be a challenging weight for 10 reps because your muscles are a little fatigued from the first set. So, try to be intuitive and pick an appropriate weight based not only on the weight you used on the previous set, but also how fatigued your muscles feel.

It is important that the weight you choose for each set challenges you for all of your desired repetitions, whether the number is 6, 8, 10, or 12 repetitions. Similarly, if you choose a weight that does not allow you to perform all the desired repetitions in good form, do as many as you can and choose a lighter weight for the next set. It is a good idea to keep a record of the weights you use on each lift so that when you perform the same exercise at another work-out you know what weight to use on each exercise set.

In general, if your goal is to get notably bigger and significantly stronger, you will want to do fewer reps with more weight, so 6-10 reps is a good target for you on most exercises. Sometimes, on exercises like the bench press and squats, even as low as 2 reps will be enough. If you are more concerned with creating muscle tone, your rep number should be in the range of 10-15. Most people's goal is a combination of muscle strength, size and tone; the target number for these folks should stay between 8-12 repetitions. Remember, however, that whether you are going for 6 reps or 15, always pick a weight that will challenge you for the full set.

Progressive Resistance

As your muscles adapt to a given exercise resistance (weight), that resistance must be gradually increased to stimulate further gains. The key to strength and muscle development is progressive resistance, which is also called "exercise progression," or "the overload principle." This is the gradual and continual addition of weight to the exercise over time, as the previous weights become too easy to lift, so that your muscles are continually forced to work harder and thus increase muscle strength, size and tone.

For example, in the Front Shoulder Press you might start out pressing (lifting) 10 kg. After two or three weeks you may find that pressing 10 kg. has become too easy, and that you can do more than your chosen number of repetitions with little or no difficulty.

The progression principle demands that as soon as the weight you are using is no longer a challenge, you must raise it. You progressively increase the weight you use for a lift so that you continue to make gains in muscle tone, size, and strength. It is important that you increase the weight only if the previous weight is too light; increasing the weight to push yourself harder can result in poor form and definitely increases the risk of injury.

Please understand that an increase in repetitions is an increase in strength. Many people think strength gains are only obtained when they increase the weight. But if you have increased the number of repetitions you can do with good form, you have increased your strength and more than likely, your muscle size and tone as well.

So, discuss exactly how to avoid the common mistake of over training. Until then, be sure to use the right amount of weight and number of repetitions for each set you do so you can achieve the results you desire.

Avoid over Training

If you feel burnt out, weak, and/or sore, you are probably over training. Not providing your muscles with enough rest will often prevent you from making improvements. Training the wrong muscle groups on consecutive days will also counteract your good results. Doing too many sets and exercises per muscle group will also cause over training.

Remember that weightlifting, especially in an intense programme, produces tissue micro trauma, those tiny tears in the muscles that temporarily decrease strength and cause varying degrees of muscle soreness. It is absolutely necessary to provide ample rest time between successive training sessions. Muscles generally require about 48 hours for the resting and rebuilding process before you work them again.

You should never train the same muscle groups on two or more days in a row (abdominals are the exception). Hypothetically then, you would do your chest, shoulders, triceps, and abdominals on Monday; on Tuesday you would train your legs, back, biceps, and abdominals; you would take Wednesday off to give all your muscle groups extra rest; on Thursday you would do chest, shoulders, triceps, and abdominals again; and on Friday you would do legs, back, biceps, and abdominals again. This would allow two days (48 hours) of rest for each muscle between training days.

Those of you who train very intensely, would benefit greatly by taking even more rest time between sessions. A week does not have to be limited to only seven days—you can expand it to eight, nine, or even ten days. Think about it: why not? Day one could consist of chest, shoulders, triceps, (pushing muscles) and abdominals on Monday.

Take Tuesday off. On day two, Wednesday, the routine could consist of legs, back, biceps, (pulling muscles) and abdominals. Take Thursday off. On Friday you do chest, shoulders, triceps, and abdominals again—and so on. This is especially important when mixing pushing and pulling muscles for different sessions. For example, if you train your chest on Monday and then triceps the next day, your triceps never really get a complete rest because they are indirectly trained with your chest on Monday and directly trained on Tuesday.

But if you split up chest/shoulders/triceps or back/biceps, working them on different days, you can implement this eight day Programme for maximum muscle resting time. Remember: always allow your muscles a chance to grow, especially when you are feeling over trained. If needed, give yourself an extra day off to grow. Never feel guilty about skipping a work-out. That extra rest could be exactly what your body needs.

Many people make the mistake of doing too many sets per exercise, and/or doing too many exercises per muscle group. It's very common for people who want great muscle size and strength gains to simply, do too much for each muscle group and over train to the point where they do more harm than good. A common weightlifting recommendation is to do at least four sets for each exercise and at least four exercises for each muscle group. This idea that "more is better" is a big misconception in the strength training industry and is recommended in many "muscle magazines" and other sources.

But when you see Mr. or Ms. Olympia in muscle magazines describing their work-outs of four to five sets per exercise and four to five exercises per muscle group, do not be fooled into thinking that if you want their results you have to do what they do. These are professional body builders, quite likely to be on steroids; they can get away with these very intense long programmes because their muscles are able to rebuild very quickly. If you are not on steroids—and for the sake of your health I hope you are not—your muscles will not be able to rebuild themselves quickly enough to make gains.

For each of the large muscle groups in the body such as back, chest, shoulders, quadriceps, and hamstrings, two to four exercises for each muscle is enough. For the smaller muscle groups such as biceps, calves, trapezius, etc., one to three exercises are enough. Because your back, for example, has specific muscles that need to be isolated, it is important that of the three exercises you perform, you do one that primarily targets each of the three areas: upper-middle back, lats, and lower back.

When you are doing two to four exercises for each muscle group, make sure you don't duplicate movements of specific muscle groups. For example, it makes no sense to do three sets of Bench Press using a barbell and then do three sets of Bench Press using dumbbells or Push-ups.

Each of these exercises requires exactly the same movement and works the same specific muscle. Instead, it would make much more sense to do bench press for overall middle chest (either barbell, dumbbell, or machine); do incline bench press for upper chest; and do dips for lower-outer chest.

One point—maybe the most important of all for ongoing strength training programmes—that is absolutely imperative to understand and implement into your training regimen is the need to overcome training plateaus. Ideally, you want to always be going through a momentum phase in which you try something new and "shock" your muscles, forcing them to make gains.

Eventually however, you will come to a point in your training where you either get bored or stop seeing results. When this happens it is absolutely crucial that you change what you are doing; this is when you need to get creative by incorporating something new into your programme. You can make effective changes in your programme in many ways: try new or alternate exercises, change the order that you train your muscles or the order of the exercises, and so forth.

You now have the knowledge to achieve the results you desire and the benefits your body deserves. Your greatest challenge, however, is not learning new exercises or the proper technique; it's not learning how many sets or reps to do or how much weight to use. Nor is it deciding when or how to change your routine.

The greatest challenge facing you at this moment is deciding whether you are willing to take action and make strength training a priority.

When you begin achieving great results, the excitement and fun you experience will make the change well worth the effort. Action creates motivation! Good luck: I hope you enjoy all the wonderful benefits of an effective strength training programme.

I mention here, a personal experience:

It was 3:00 a.m. when the phone suddenly rang out in the darkness. Upon answering, a voice cried out, "This is your brother, Dad just died of a heart attack. The paramedics are on the way." I was completely shocked. I had seen my father a few days earlier, and there weren't any indications that he was ill. In fact, he appeared to be in peak form. Confused and grief stricken, I began to search for the cause of his death. I suspected that it was his "no activity" lifestyle and high fat diet that finally caught up with him.

The next day, the coroner's report confirmed my suspicion: His death was the result of atherosclerosis, a narrowing of the arteries from deposits of cholesterol and fat. The truth was painful. Especially, when the experts concluded that his premature death could have been completely avoided—only if he had the appropriate medical care. It became very clear, that it was his bad habits which ultimately robbed him of his life. Now, he's gone and never to return.

Regretfully, when I look back and ask "Why didn't he save himself?" The answer was obvious: He was in denial, he lacked knowledge about health, and would not accept that he had a life threatening problem.

Yes, bad habits can kill, but it is possible to change your lifestyle. However, it requires an entirely different mindset: First, you must take personal responsibility for your own health. Second, develop the awareness that you need to make definite changes in your life.

Third, educate yourself and learn the fundamental premises of good health. Forth, research the health risks that are associated with aging; and Fifth, inquire into your family's history of diseases and pathology. Armed with these facts, you now have the basics to make informed decisions about the nutritional and exercise requirements that you need.

Nevertheless, changing life long habits is not an easy task. Typically, desperate family members quote medical statistics and use scare tactics to try and change their loved ones. It simply does not work. To make matters worse, pressuring and nagging creates even more resistance. If anything, it erects a wall of denial which can defy all rational explanations regarding good health. The usual reaction is "that could never happen to me.". When it does—it can be fatal.

Then, what is the answer? To get someone to change their deeply entrenched habits requires their conscious commitment to take personal responsibility for their own life. There is no other way! The problem is, that the onset of most diseases of aging are silent killers. They are slow, progressive and insidious. There are no warning signs, no pains nor any pronounced symptoms that would hint to an impending disaster. This is typical of heart disease, stroke, and cancer in individuals over the age of fifty. For that reason, it's no surprise that many people do not make the connection that today's lifestyle habits can potentially lead to premature death. Therefore, if you are risking your health by poor habits—this is what you can do to change.

Primarily, you need to understand the nature of habits, and what makes them so difficult to change. Clinical Psychologist, John F. Tristany, Ph.D. defines habits as, "deeply ingrained, learned patterns of behaviour that are continually reinforced by environmental, emotional, and psychological factors." He continues, "habits are maintained by the Pleasure Principal: the desire to gain pleasure and the absolute need to avoid pain".

To understand how the pleasure principal is applied to changes in exercise, diet, and lifestyle—it must be compared to the sedentary individual. For these people, physical activity is alien. Exercise, aerobics, and muscle fatigue are interpreted by the brain as pain provoking. The result is pain avoidance, withdrawal and alternative pleasure seeking. This is where searching for passive stimulation such as overeating, drugs, alcohol, and sex are anchored to the pleasure principal; and therefore, reinforce inactivity.

Dr. Tristany believes that this principal is reversed for active people. He states, "physical exertion is emotionally associated with good health, strength, and body image. The pain impulses linked to exercise become positively associated to one's physical identity and to the euphoria of sexual attractiveness. Thus, the habits of a healthy lifestyle are rewarded by the pleasure principal through social recognition and physical feelings of well-being.

The same principal applies to eating behaviours as well. Most people react to dieting as a negative experience to be avoided. Food restriction is felt to be depriving, frustrating and painful for most. Giving up those sweet and creamy foods, stemming from old family habits, is truly a painful experience. Conversely, those who value fitness—associate pain with consuming fattening foods.

They experience discomfort just thinking about being overweight or potentially compromising their health. These examples may seem simplistic; but if you think about your food preferences, you will begin to recognise how this principal affects your attitudes, thoughts and behaviours.

Understanding your philosophy of life is the next critical step towards changing your habits. Lifestyle patterns such as attitudes and fixed habits of inactivity fall into this category. As defined by Clinical Psychologist, Joseph Nicolosi, Ph.D., "A philosophy of life is a global and all encompassing view of the world. One's attitudes and beliefs are shaped from childhood experiences as a reaction to their role model's consequences. Moreover, these beliefs are felt to be absolutely true, and take on life directing consequences for one's behaviour."

Dr. Nicolosi cites the example of a hedonist whose view of life is to obtain as much pleasure as possible and to avoid all unpleasant feelings. He states, "A child who loses a parent at an early age may develop the belief of, 'live today for there maybe no tomorrow."' Clearly, this child losing a parent is a rarity, but for this little person it was a painful reality. Nicolosi concludes, "such individuals may develop an over indulgent personality that only seeks pleasure, convenience, and effortlessness in order to compensate for such an early and devastating loss."

According to Dr. Tristany, "a belief system supports and validates an individual's philosophy of life. These beliefs, derived from early learning, take on 'religious like convictions' which are felt to be 'the absolute truth.' Thereafter, these conceptual absolutes become life directing."

He warns that, "Belief systems are not always valid, nor do they necessarily correspond with reality." This is where inaccurate beliefs can get an individual into serious and life-threatening trouble.

Undoubtedly, misbeliefs can steer your life in the wrong direction. As a personal trainer, part of my clientele consists of overweight individuals that are "at risk" for heart disease. One sixty year old client believed that eating egg yolk was the secret to long life. All was well—until she started having chest pains. Her cardiological exam revealed that she had coronary artery disease.

The doctor recommended: lose 22 kg., change your diet, and start an exercise programme; otherwise, the results could be fatal. The moral of the story is that the right information can save your life.